AN INTRODUCTION TO MADHYAMAKA PHILOSOPHY

An Introduction to
Madhyamaka Philosophy

Jaidev Singh

MOTILAL BANARSIDASS PUBLISHERS
PRIVATE LIMITED • DELHI

*5th Reprint: Delhi, **2016***
Second Revised Edition: Delhi, 1976
First Edition: Varanasi, 1968

ISBN: 978-81-208-0326-8

MOTILAL BANARSIDASS
41 U.A., Bungalow Road, Jawahar Nagar, Delhi 110 007
8 Mahalaxmi Chamber, 22 Bhulabhai Desai Road, Mumbai 400 026
203 Royapettah High Road, Mylapore, Chennai 600 004
236, 9th Main III Block, Jayanagar, Bangaluru 560 011
8 Camac Street, Kolkata 700 017
Ashok Rajpath, Patna 800 004
Chowk, Varanasi 221 001

Printed in India

by RP Jain at NAB Printing Unit,
A-44, Naraina Industrial Area, Phase I, New Delhi–110028
and published by JP Jain for Motilal Banarsidass Publishers (P) Ltd,
41 U.A. Bungalow Road, Jawahar Nagar, Delhi-110007

PREFACE

This is a brief Introduction to Madhyamaka Philosophy. It contains, however, all the essential features of this system.

It gives a history of the rise and growth of Madhyamaka Philosophy, and the origin, structure, development and purpose of the Madhyamaka dialectic. It elucidates in detail the distinction between Hīnayāna and Mahāyāna in respect of *pratītyasamutpāda*, *nirvāṇa*, the ideal of religious discipline, the concept of Dharma, and the concept of Buddhology.

It discusses in detail the meaning of Śūnya-Śūnyatā and its axiological and soteriological significance.

Other important features of the Introduction are the clarification of the concept of Madhyamā Pratipad, Saṁvṛti and Paramārtha Satya, Tathatā, Dharmadhātu and Bhūtakoṭi. It gives not only the negative side of Nāgārjuna's Philosophy but also his positive contribution.

With all these features, this Introduction will be of value to the students of Madhyamaka Philosophy.

Jaideva Singh

CONTENTS

INTRODUCTION

Mahāyāna and Hīnayāna

There are two aspects of Mahāyāna Philosophy, viz. the Madhyamaka Philosophy or Śūnyavāda and Yogācāra or Vijñānavāda. Here we are concerned only with Madhyamaka Philosophy or Śūnyavāda.

Generally there are three names current for Hīnayāna and Mahāyāna. The three names for the former are Southern Buddhism, Original Buddhism, and Hīnayāna, and those for the latter Northern Buddhism, Developed Buddhism and Mahāyāna. The first two names are given by European scholars. Southern and Northern Buddhism are names used on Geographical basis. European scholars called Buddhism prevalent in countries to the north of India, viz., Nepal, Tibet, China, Japan etc., Northern Buddhism and that prevalent in countries to the South of India, viz., Ceylon, Burma, Siam etc. Southern Buddhism. This division is not quite correct, for, according to Dr. J. Takakusu, the Buddhism prevalent in Java and Sumatra which lie in a southern direction from India is similar to that prevalent in the North.

The division 'original and developed Buddhism' is based on the belief that Mahāyāna was only a gradual development of the original doctrine which was Hīnayāna, but this is not acceptable to Mahāyānists. Japanese scholars maintain that the great Buddha imparted his teachings to his pupils according to their receptive capacities. To some he imparted his exoteric teachings (*vyakta-upadeśa*) containing his 'phenomenological perception;' to more advanced pupils he imparted his subtle esoteric teachings (*guhya-upadeśa*) containing his 'ontological perception.' The Buddha generally gave an outline of both the teachings, and both were developed by the great *ācāryas*. It is, therefore, a misnomer to call one 'original Buddhism' and another 'developed Buddhism.' Both the teachings were delivered simultaneously. The exoteric teachings may be called well-known Buddhism and the esoteric less known, the latter being subtler than the former.

We have, however, to find out how the terms Hīnayāna and Mahāyāna came into vogue. According to R. Kimura, the Mahāsaṅghikas had retained the esoteric teachings of the Buddha and were more liberal and advanced than the Sthaviras. In the Vaisāli Council, the Mahāsaṅghikas or the Vajjian monks were excommunicated by the Sthaviras for expressing opinions different from those of the orthodox school, and were denounced as 'Pāpa Bhikkhus' and 'Adhammavādins.' The Mahāsaṅghikas, in order to show the superiority of their doctrines over those of the Sthaviras, coined the term Mahāyāna (the higher vehicle) for their own school, and Hīnayāna (the lower vehicle) for the school of their opponents. Thus the terms Mahāyāna and Hīnayāna came into vogue. It goes without saying that these terms were used only by the Mahāyānists.

Three Phases in Buddhism

Three phases can be easily marked in Buddhist philosophy and religion.

1. *The Ābhidharmic phase from the Buddha's death to Ist Century A. D.*

This was the realistic and pluralistic phase of Buddhism. The method of this school was one of analysis. The philosophy of this period consisted mostly of analysis of psycho-physical phenomena into *dharmas* (elements) *saṁskṛta* (compounded or conditioned) and *asaṁskṛta* (uncompounded or unconditioned). The main interest in this period was psychological-soteriological. The dominant tone of this school was one of rationalism combined with meditation practices. The language used in this period was Pāli, and the school is known as Hīnayāna.

2. *Development of Esoteric Teachings*

The second phase consisted of the development of the esoteric teachings of the Buddha which were current among the Mahāsaṅghikas, simultaneously with the Ābhidharmic phase. The main interest in this period was ontological-soteriological. The dominant tone of this school was one of supra-rationalism combined with *yoga*. The main attempt was to find out the *Svabhāva* or true nature of Reality and to realize it in oneself by developing Prajñā. The language used was Saṁskṛta or mixed Saṁskṛta. This school was known as Mahāyāna. The earlier phase was known as Madhyamaka philosophy or Śūnyavāda, the later as Yogācāra or Vijñānavāda. This phase lasted from 2nd century A.D. to 500 A.D.

3. *Development of Tantra*

The third phase was that of Tantra. This lasted from 500 A. D. to 1000 A.D. The main interest of the period was cosmical-soteriological. The dominant feature of this school was occultism. The main emphasis was on adjustment and harmony with the cosmos and on achieving enlightenment by *mantric* and occult methods. The language was mostly Saṁskṛta and Apabhraṁśa. The main Tāntric schools were Mantrayāna, Vajrayāna, Sahajayāna, Kālacakrayāna.

Here we are not concerned with the first and third phase. We are concerned only with the earlier phase of the second period. Stcherbatsky has provided a translation only of the first and twentyfifth chapters i.e. the chapter dealing with causality and that dealing with Nirvāṇa of the Madhyamaka Śāstra or the Madhyamaka-Kārikās of Nāgārjuna together with the commentary of Candrakīrti. In the Introduction, an attempt is made to give a brief resumè of the Madhyamaka system as a whole.

Madhyamaka Śāstra : life of Nāgārjuna and Āryadeva

The Madhyamaka philosophy is contained mainly in the Madhyamaka Śāstra of Nāgārjuna and the *Catuḥ-Śataka* of Āryadeva.

Books on Mahāyāna Buddhism were completely lost in India. Their translation existed in Chinese, Japanese and Tibetan. Mahāyāna literature was written mostly in Saṁskrta and mixed Saṁskṛta. Scholars who had made a study of Buddhism hardly suspected that there were books on Buddhism in Saṁskṛta also.

Mr. Brian Houghton Hodgson was appointed Resident at Kāṭhamāṇḍu in Nepal in 1833, and served in this capacity up to the end of 1843.

During this period, he discovered there 381 bundles of

manuscripts on Buddhism in Saṁskṛta. These were distributed to various learned societies for editing and publication. It was then found out that the Buddhism in the Saṁskṛta manuscripts was greatly different from that of the Pāli Canon, and that the Buddhism in China, Japan, Tibet etc. was very much similar to that of the Saṁskṛta works. Among the Saṁskṛta manuscripts was also found the *Madhyamakaśāstra* of Nāgārjuna together with the commentary known as *Prasannapadā* by Candrakīrti. This was edited by Louis de la Valleè-Poussin and published in the *Bibliotheca Buddhica*, Vol. IV. St. Petersburg, Russia in 1912. An earlier edition of this book was published by the Buddhist Text Society, Calcutta, in 1897 and edited by Śaraccandra Śāstrī. This was full of misprints. Poussin consulted this book, but he also used two other manuscripts, one from Cambridge and another from Paris. He also checked up the text of the Kārikās and the commentary with the help of Tibetan translation. Dr. P. L. Vaidya utilised Poussin's edition and brought out in 1960 *Madhyamaka Śāstra* of Nāgārjuna with Candrakīrti's commentary in Devanāgarī character. This has been published by Mithilā Vidyāpīṭha, Darbhaṅgā. Stcherbatsky had utilized Poussin's edition in writing out his Conception of Buddhist Nirvāṇa.

The Buddha used to characterize his teaching as *madhyamā-pratipad* (the middle path). When Nāgārjuna evolved his philosophy, he seized upon this important word, and called his philosophy *Madhyamaka* (*madhyamaiva madhyamakam*) or *Madhyamaka-śāstra*. The followers of this system came to be known as Mādhyamika (*madhyamakam adhīyate vidanti vā Mādhyamikāḥ*). The correct name for the system is Madhyamaka, not Mādhyamika. Mādhyamika means the believer in or follower of the Madhyamaka system.

Under the title of *Madhyamaka-śāstra*, Nāgārjuna wrote out his philosophical teaching in over 400 *kārikās* in *anuṣṭubha* metre, divided into 27 chapters.

Nāgārjuna

He was the teacher who developed and perfected the Madhyamaka system. He flourished in the second century A.D.

He was born in a Brahmin family in Āndhradeśa probably in Vidarbha (Berār). Śrīparvata and Dhānyakaṭaka were the centres of his activities in the south. In the north, he carried on his activities in many places of which Nālandā is said to be the most prominent. He was also connected with Amarāvatī and Nāgārjunakoṇḍa. *Rājataraṅgiṇī* (11th Century A.D.) says that he was a contemporary of Huṣka, Juṣka and Kaniṣka.

According to the biography of Nāgārjuna, translated into Chinese by Kumārajīva (about 405 A.D.), Nāgārjuna was born in a Brahmin family in Southern India, and studied the Vedas and other important branches of Brāhmanical learning. He was later converted to Buddhism.

One of his minor works, *Suhṛllekha* (Friendly Epistle) is said to have been addressed to the Āndhra king, Śātavāhana. Śātavāhana is, however, regarded not as the name of a particular king, but as the name of a family of Āndhra kings, founded by Simuka (vide, *Ancient India*, by R. C. Majumdar, p. 133). Some scholars maintain that *Suhṛllekha* was addressed to Kaniṣka.

There is a legend associated with his name. Nāga means a serpent or dragon. Arjuna is the name of a tree. It is said that he was born under an Arjuna tree, and he visited the submarine kingdom of the Nāgas, where the Nāga king transmitted to him the *Mahāprajñāpāramitā Sūtra* which had been entrusted to the Nāgas by the Buddha.

The word 'Nāga' however, is symbolic of wisdom. The Buddha is said to have remarked, "The serpent is a name for one who has destroyed the *āsavas* (passions)" (*Majjhima-Nikāya*, I.23.). The Nāgas may, therefore, have been certain Arhants to whom the *prajñāpāramitā* teachings may have been handed down. Nāgārjuna may have received the teachings from them.

The Buddhist Nāgārjuna should not be confused with the Chemist and Tāntrika Nāgārjuna who lived probably in the 7th century A.D.

The Tibetans ascribe 122 books to Nāgārjuna, but only the following seem to have been his authentic works.

(1) *Madhyamaka-Śāstra*, also known as Prajñā or Kārikās with the commentary, *Akutobhaya* by the author himself

(2) *Vigrahavyāvartanī* with a commentary by the author.
(3) *Yuktiṣaṣṭikā.*
(4) *Śūnyatā-saptati* with a commentary by the author.
(5) *Pratītyasamutpādahṛdaya* with a commentary.
(6) *Catuḥstava.*
(7) *Bhāvanākrama.*
(8) *Suhṛllekha.*
(9) *Bhāvasamkrānti.*
(10) *Ratnāvalī.*
(11) *Prajñāpāramitā-sūtra-Śāstra.*
(12) *Daśabhūmivibhāṣā-śāstra.*
(13) *Eka-śloka-śāstra.*
(14) *Vaidalya sūtra* and *Prakaraṇa.*
(15) *Vyavahāra-siddhi.*

Only a few of these are available in the original. There is, however, a Tibetan translation of all these books.

Kumārajīva's biography of Nāgārjuna mentions the following works also as Nāgārjuna's.

1. Upadeśa in 100,000 gāthās 2. Buddhamārgālaṅkāraśāstra in 5,000 gāthās 3. Akutobhaya-śāstra in 100,000 gāthās.

The Chinese collection mentions the following also among the works of Nāgārjuna :

1. Mahāyānabhavabheda-śāstra (bhavasaṅkrāntiśāstra) 2. Buddhisambhāra-śāstra 3. Dharmadhātustava.

Āryadeva or Ārya Deva

He was born in Siṁhala (Ceylon) and became a pupil of Nāgārjuna. He travelled with him to various places and helped him greatly in propagating his doctrine.

His biography was translated into Chinese by Kumārajīva in about 405 A.D.

His most famous work is *Catuḥ-Śataka* which consists of 400 Kārikās. He defended the teachings of Nāgārjuna, and criticized the philosophy of Hīnayāna, Sāṁkhya and Vaiśeṣika. He was probably the author of *Akṣara-Śatakaṃ.* He is also said to have been the author of *Hastavala-prakaraṇa* and *Cittaviśuddhi-prakaraṇa.* Prof. Winternitz expresses his doubt whether *Citta-viśuddhi-prakaraṇa* was his work.

It is said that he was murdered by the pupil of a heretical teacher whom he had defeated in disputation.

The Original Sources of Mahāyāna

The origin of Mahāyāna may be traced to an earlier school known as *Mahāsaṅghika* and earlier literary sources known as *Mahāyāna sūtras*.

1. *Mahāsaṅghikas*

At the council held at Vaisāli (according to Kimura) certain monks differed widely from the opinions of other monks on certain important points of the *dharma*. Though the monks that differed formed the majority, they were excommunicated by the others who called them 'Pāpa Bhikkhus and Adhammavādins'. In Buddhist history, these Bhikkhus were known as *Mahāsaṅghikas,* because they formed the majority at the council or probably because they reflected the opinions of the larger section of the laity. The Bhikkhus who excommunicated them styled themselves Sthaviras or the Elders, because they believed that they represented the original, orthodox doctrine of the Buddha. We have seen that the *Mahāsaṅghikas* coined the term *Mahāyāna* to represent their system of belief and practice, and called the Sthaviras' *Hīnayāna.*

Let us see what the main tenets of the *Mahāsaṅghikas* were. Their contributions can be summed up under four heads.

1. *The Status of the Buddha*

According to the Mahāsaṅghikas, the Buddha was not simply a historical person. The real Buddha was transcendental, supramundane, eternal, and infinite. The historical Buddha was only a fictitious person sent by Him to appear in the world, to assume a human body, to live like an ordinary human being and teach the *dharma* to the inhabitants of the world. The real Buddha is the Reality *par excellence* and will continue to send messengers to the world to teach the true *dharma* to mankind.

2. *The Status of the Arhat*

The *Sthaviras* had attributed perfection to the Arhats.

The *Mahāsaṅghikas* maintained that the Arhats were not perfect; they were troubled by doubts and were ignorant of many things. They should not be held up as ideals. Rather those should be emulated as ideals who during aeons of self-sacrifice and struggle attained to Buddhahood.

3. *The Status of Empirical knowledge*

According to the *Mahāsaṅghikas*, empirical knowledge could not give us an insight into Reality. Only *Śūnyatā* which transcends all worldly things can give us a vision of the Real. All verbal statements give us a false view of the Real; they are mere thought-constructs.

4. *The Unsubstantial Nature of the Dharmas*

The Sthaviras believed that the *pudgala* or a personal self was unsubstantial, but the *dharmas* or elements of existence were real entities. The Mahāsaṅghikas maintained that not only were the *pudgalas* unsubstantial (*pudgala-nairātmya*), but the *dharmas* (elements of existence) were also unsubstantial (*dharma-nairātmya*). Every thing was unsubstantial (*śūnya*).

It will be seen from the above account that the germs of practically all the important tenets of Madhyamaka philosophy were present in the system of the Mahāsaṅghikas.

It is the *Mahāsaṅghikas* who first of all gave expression to Buddha's ontological perceptions which were first embodied in the Mahāyāna sūtras and were later developed into Mahāyāna philosophy and religion.

11. *Literary Sources*

In Buddhism, *sūtra* literature is said to contain the direct, oral teachings of the Buddha, and *śāstra* is said to contain the scholarly and philosophical elaboration of the direct teachings of the Buddha.

We have a large bulk of literary works known as *Mahāyāna sūtras*. Being *sūtras*, they claim to be the direct teachings of the Buddha. Such bulky volumes, obviously, cannot be the spoken word of the Buddha. They are the elaboration of some 'seminal sūtras' which are so deeply embedded in the voluminous *Mahāyāna sūtra* literature that it is now almost impossible to disentangle them.

The most important of these works are the *prajñāpāramitā sūtras. Prajñā-pāramitā* is generally translated as 'perfect wisdom.' The word 'pāram-itā' i.e. 'gone beyond' suggests that it would be better to translate *prajñā-pāramitā* as 'transcendent insight' or 'transcendent wisdom'. The Tibetans translate it in this way. In all countries where Mahāyāna is a living religion, the following *prajñā-pāramitā mantra* is generally recited: *Gate, gate, pāraṁgate, pārasaṁgate Bodhi, svāhā* i.e. "O wisdom which has gone beyond the beyond, to thee Homage."

According to Dr. Edward Conze, the composition of the *Prajñā pāramitā* texts extended over about a thousand years which may be divided into four phases.

The first phase (C. 100 B. C. to A.D. 100) consists in the elaboration of the teaching in a basic text.

The second phase (C.A.D. 100-300) consists in the expansion of the teaching into three or four lengthy treatises.

The third phase (C.A.D. 300-500) consists in the abridgement of the teachings into a few shorter treatises.

The fourth phase (C. A. D. 500-1200) consists in its condensation into Tāntric *dhāraṇīs* and *mantras*.

(1) According to most scholars, the *Aṣṭa sāhasrikā*, consisting of 8,000 lines is the oldest of the *Prajñāpāramitā* literature. It had its origin probably among the Mahāsaṅghikas. The principal theme of this treatise is the doctrine of *śūnyatā* (void or emptiness).

(2) *Aṣṭa-sāhasrikā* seems to have been expanded in the three hundred years that followed into *Śatasāhasrikā* (of 100,000 lines), *Pañcaviṁśatisāhasrikā* (of 25,000 lines) and *Aṣṭādaśasāhasrikā* (of 18,000 lines). The last one was translated by Lokarakṣa in A. D. 172.

(3) Now began the abridgement of the *Prajñā-pāramitā* literature. The earliest abridgements are the *Hṛdaya-sūtra* and the *Vajracchedikā sūtra*. The *Vajracchedikā* was translated into Chinese probably in the 5th century A. D. This translation was printed in China on 11th May, 868. This is said to be the oldest printed book in the world.

Abhisamayālaṁkāra is said to be a summary of *pañcaviṁśatisāhasrikā* made by Maitreyanātha, the teacher of Asaṅga.

(4) Lastly *Prajñāpāramitā* was condensed into *dhāraṇīs* and *mantras*. One of these, viz., *Ekākṣarī* says that the perfec-

tion of wisdom is contained only in one letter, viz., 'a'. Ultimately *Prajñāpāramitā* was personified as a goddess to be worshipped.

Prajñāpāramitās are both philosophy and religion. They are not mere 'philosophy' in the Western sense of the word. In the West, philosophy cut itself adrift from religion and became a purely intellectual pursuit. In India, every philosophy was a religion, and every religion had a philosophy. Western religion became only a credal religion. Indian religion was a philosophical religion.

The principal theme of the *Prajñāpāramitā* literature is the doctrine of *śūnyatā*. The Hīnayānists believed only in *pudgala-nairātmya* or the unsubstantiality of the individual. They classified Reality into certain *dharmas* or elements of existence and thought that the *dharmas* were substantially real. *Prajñā-pāramitā* gives a knock-out to this belief. It teaches *sarva-dharma-śūnyatā*, the unsubstantiality of all *dharmas*.

Phenomena are dependent on conditions. Being so dependent, they are devoid of substantial reality. Hence they are *śūnya* (empty).

Nirvāṇa being transcendent to all categories of thought is *Śūnyatā* (emptiness) itself.

Both *saṁsāra* and *Nirvāṇa*, the conditioned and unconditioned are mere thought-constructs and are so devoid of reality.

Ultimate Reality may be called *Śūnyatā* in the sense that it transcends all empirical determinations and thought-constructs.

Prajñā or transcendent insight consists in ceasing to indulge in thought-constructs. So *Prajñā* becomes synonymous with *Śūnyatā*.

One, however, acquires insight into *Śūnyatā* not merely by avowing it enthusiastically, nor by logomachy, but by meditation on *Śūnyatā*.

One has to meditate on *Śūnyatā* as the absence of self-hood, on the absence of substantiality in all the *dharmas*, on *Śūnyatā* as even the emptiness of the unconditioned. Finally one has to abandon *Śūnyatā* itself as a mere raft to cross the ocean of ignorance. This meditation will, however, be ineffective unless one has cultivated certain moral virtues.

Though this is a very brief summary of the *Prajñāpāramitā* texts, it is enough to show that this kind of literature contained all the important elements of the Mahāyāna system.

Thus we see that the Madhyamaka system was developed on the basis of the doctrines of the *Mahāsaṅghikas* and the *Mahāyāna sūtras* known as *Prajñāpāramitā sūtras.*

The Madhyamaka Works and Schools

The Madhyamaka system of philosophy was developed mainly by Nāgārjuna. He was one of the greatest geniuses the world has ever known. The system of which he laid the foundation was developed by his brilliant followers. It had a continuous history of development from the second century A.D. upto eleventh century A.D.

Three stages of its development can be easily marked. In the first stage, there was a systematic formulation of the Madhyamaka philosophy by Nāgārjuna and Āryadeva. The second stage is one of division of the system into two schools the *Prāsaṅgika* and the *Svātantrika.* The third stage is one of re-affirmation of the *Prāsaṅgika* school.

Nāgārjuna and Āryadeva (2nd Century A. D.)

First Stage—Nāgārjuna was the author of a voluminous commentary on *Prajñāpāramitā* known as *Prajñāpāramitā-śāstra.* This was translated into Chinese by Kumārajīva (A. D. 402-405). The original is not available now. He, however, formulated his main philosophy in *prajñā-mūla* or *Mūla-Madhyamaka-Kārikās* known also as Madhyamaka-Śāstra. His devoted pupil Āryadeva elaborated his philosophy in *Catuḥ-śataka.* We have already seen what other books were written by Nāgārjuna and Āryadeva.

Second stage—Nāgārjuna had used the technique of *prasaṅga* in formulating his Madhyamaka philosophy. *Prasaṅga* is a technical word which means *reductio ad absurdum* argument. Nāgārjuna did not advance any theory of his own, and therefore, had no need to advance any argument to prove his theory. He used only *prasaṅga-vākya* or *reductio ad absurdum* argument to prove that the theories advanced by his opponents only led to absurdity on the very principles accepted by them. This implied that Reality was beyond thought- constructs.

Buddhapālita who flourished in the middle of the sixth century was an ardent follower of Nāgārjuna. He felt that *prasaṅga* was the correct method of the Madhyamaka philosophy and employed it in his teachings and writings. He wrote a commentary called *Madhyamakavṛtti* on the *Madhyamaka Śāstra* of Nāgārjuna. This is available only in Tibetan translation. The original is lost.

A junior contemporary of Buddhapālita, named Bhavya or Bhāvaviveka maintained that the opponent should not only be reduced to absurdity, but *svatantra* or independent logical arguments should also be advanced to silence him. He believed that the system of dialectics alone could not serve the purpose of pin-pointing the Absolute Truth.

He wrote *Mahāyāna-Karatala-ratna Śāstra*, *Mādhyamikahṛdaya* with an auto-commentary, called *Tarkajvālā*, *Madhyamārtha-Saṁgraha* and *Prajñā-pradīpa*, a commentary on the Madhyamaka Śāstra of Nāgārjuna. Only a Tibetan translation of these works is available. Dr. L. M. Joshi transcribed the *Madhyamārtha-Saṁgraha* into Nāgarī letters and translated it into Hindi which appeared in the *Dharmadūta*, Vol. 29, July-August, 1964.

N. Aiyswāmi Śāstri has restored *Karatalaratna* from the Chinese translation of Yuan Chwang into Saṁskṛta (Viśvabhārati Śantiniketan, 1949).

So we see that in the sixth century, nearly 400 years after the death of Nāgārjuna, the Madhyamaka school was split into two, viz. (a) Prāsaṅgika school, led by Buddhapālita and (b) Svātantrika School, led by Bhāvaviveka.

Y. Kajiama says that the problem which divided the Mādhyamikas was whether the system of relative knowledge could be recognised as valid or not, though it was delusive from the absolute point of view.

According to Yuan Chwang, Bhāvaviveka externally wore the Sāṁkhya cloak, though internally he was supporting the doctrine of Nāgārjuna.

Third Stage—In the third stage, we have two very brilliant scholars of the Madhyamaka system, viz. Candrakīrti and Śāntideva.

A large number of commentaries (about twenty) was written on Nāgārjuna's Madhyamaka Śāstra. They are available only in Tibetan translation. Candrakīrti's *prasannapadā* commentary is the only one that has survived in the original Saṁskṛta. It seems to have elbowed every other commentary out of existence.

He flourished early in the seventh century A. D. and wrote several works. He was born in Samanta in the South. He studied Madhyamaka philosophy under Kamalabuddhi, a disciple of Buddhapālita and probably under Bhavya also. His *prasannapadā* commentary on Nāgārjuna's *Madhyamaka Śāstra*, has already been mentioned. He wrote an independent work, named *Madhyamakāvatāra* with an auto-commentary. He frequently refers to *Madhyamakāvatāra* in his *Prasannapadā* which goes to show that the former was written earlier than the latter.

He also wrote commentaries on Nāgārjuna's *Śūnyatā Saptati* and *Yukti Ṣaṣṭikā* and on Āryadeva's *Catuḥśataka*. Two other *prakaraṇas* or manuals, viz., *Madhyamakaprajñāvatāra* and *Pañcaskandha* were also written by him. Of all his works, only *Prasannapadā* is available in the original; other works are available only in Tibetan translation.

Candrakīrti vigorously defends the *Prāsaṅgika* school, and exposes the hollowness of Bhāvaviveka's logic at many places.

He also supports the common-sense view of sense-perception and criticizes the doctrine of the 'unique particular' (*svalakṣaṇa*) and perception devoid of determination (*kalpanāpoḍha*).

He has also criticized Vijñānavāda and maintains that consciousness (*vijñāna*) without an object is unthinkable.

Śāntideva was another great pillar of the *Prāsaṅgika* school. He flourished in the seventh century A. D. According to Tārānātha, Śāntideva was the son of King Kalyāṇavarman of Saurāṣṭra and was the rightful successor to the throne. As a prince he was known as Śāntivarman. He was so deeply inspired by Mahāyānic ideal that he fled away from his kingdom and took orders with Jaideva in Nālandā after which he was known as Śāntideva.

He was the author of *Śikṣā-samuccaya* and *Bodhicaryāvatāra*. In the former, he has referred to many important Mahāyāna works, nearly 97 in number which are now completely lost. In the *Bodhicaryāvatāra* he has emphasized the cultivation of Bodhicitta. He was the greatest poet of the Madhyamaka school and his works evince a beautiful fusion of poetry and philosophy. He was the follower of the *Prāsaṅgika* method and has criticized Vijñānavāda vehemently.

It may be said in passing that Śāntarakṣita and Kamalaśīla represent a syncretism of the Madhyamaka system and Vijñānavāda and cannot be strictly called Mādhyamikas. Śāntarakṣita flourished in the eighth century A. D. His great work was *Tattvasaṁgraha* (Compendium of Reality). His celebrated pupil, Kamalaśīla wrote the *Tattvasaṁgraha-pañjikā*, a learned commentary on *Tattvasaṁgraha.*

The Madhyamaka Dialectic : Its Origin, Structure And Development.

We have seen that nearly all the important tenets of the Madhyamaka philosophy were already adumbrated in the Mahāsaṅghika system and *Prajñāpāramitā* literature. Nāgārjuna only developed them. What was then the original contribution of Nāgārjuna? His original contribution was the dialectic that he evolved. He certainly threw new light on the various doctrines of Mahāyāna foreshadowed in the Mahāsaṅghika thought and *Prajñāpāramitā* works, and provided a deeper and more critical exposition of those doctrines, but his most original contribution was the dialectic.

The mysterious silence of the Buddha on the most fundamental questions of Metaphysics led him to probe into the reason of that silence. Was the Buddha agnostic as some of the European writers on Buddhism believe him to be? If not, what was the reason of his silence? Through a searching inquiry into this silence was the dialectic born.

There are well-known questions which the Buddha declared to be *avyākṛta* i.e. the answers to which were inexpressible. Candrakīrti enumerates them in his commentary on the MK, 22, 12.

He begins by saying *Iha caturdaśa avyākṛta-vastūni bhagavatā nirdiṣṭāni*—The Lord announced fourteen things to be inexpressible," and then mentions them in the following order:

(1) Whether the world is (a) eternal, (b) or not, (c) or both (d) or neither-4

(2) Whether the world is (a) finite, (b) infinite, (c) or both, (d) or neither-4

(3) Whether the Tathāgata (a) exists after death, (b) or does not, (c) or both, (d) or neither-4

(4) Whether the soul is identical with the body or different from it-2 = 14 in all.

It will be seen that there are four alternatives in the first three sets of questions. There could be four alternatives in the last question also. These four alternatives formed the basis of *Catuṣkoṭi* or tetra-lemma of Nāgārjuna's dialectic. In each, there is (i) a positive thesis, opposed by (ii) a negative counter-thesis. These two are the basic alternatives. (iii) They are conjunctively affirmed to form the third alternative, and (iv) disjunctively denied to form the fourth.

The 'yes' or 'no' answer to these fundamental questions could not do justice to truth. Buddha called such speculations mere *diṭṭhivāda* and refused to be drawn into them.

Nāgārjuna had before him the structure of these questions and Buddha's silence, refusing to give any categorical answer to such questions. Buddha used to say that he neither believed in *Śāśvata-vāda*, an absolute affirmation, nor in *Ucchedavāda* an absolute negation. His position was one of *madhyamā pratipada* (literally, the middle position).

Nāgārjuna pondered deeply over this attitude of the Buddha, and came to the conclusion that the reason of Buddha's studied silence in regard to such questions was that Reality was transcendent to thought. He systematized the four alternatives (*antas* or *koṭis*), mercilessly exposed the disconcerting implications of each alternative, brought the antinomies of Reason luminously to the fore by hunting them out from every cover, and demonstrated the impossibility of erecting a sound Metaphysic on the basis of dogmatism or rationalism. This was his dialectic. The four alternatives were already formulated by the Buddha. His originality consisted in drawing out by the application of rigorous logic the implications of each alternative, driving Reason in a *cul de sac* and thus preparing the mind for taking a right-about-turn (*parāvṛtti*) towards *prajñā*.

To the unwary reader, Nāgārjuna appears to be either a cantankerous philosopher out to controvert all systems, or as a sophist trickster wringing from an unsuspecting opponent certain concessions in argument by artful equivocation and then chuckling over his discomfiture or as a destructive nihilist negativing every view brusquely, affirming none.

On a more careful study of his dialectic, it will appear that none of these fears is true, that he is, in all soberness, only trying to show up the inevitable conflict in which Reason gets involved when it goes beyond its legitimate province of comprehending phenomena, and enters the forbidden land of noumena.

The Meaning of Dialectic

What then does dialectic mean? In plain words, dialectic is that movement of thought which, by examining the *pros* and *cons* of a question, brings about a clear consciousness of the antinomies into which Reason gets bogged up, and hints at a way out of the impasse by rising to a plane higher than Reason.

Structure of The Dialectic

We have seen that the origin of the dialectic of the Mādhyamika lay in the four alternatives in each *avyākṛta* problem followed by a mysterious silence on the part of the Buddha. Nāgārjuna clearly systematized these and formulated them into the *catuṣkoṭi*, tetralemma or quadrilemma, also called the four-cornered negation. The structure of the clearly articulated dialectic finally stood thus:

The first alternative of the tetralemma consisted of (i) a positive thesis, the second of (ii) a negative counter-thesis, the third of (iii) a conjunctive affirmation of the first two, the fourth of (iv) a disjunctive denial of the first two.

The Technique of The Dialectic

The technique of the dialectic consisted in drawing out the implications of the view of the opponent on the basis of the principles accepted by himself and thus showing the self-contradictory character of that view. The opponent was hoisted with his own petard. He was reduced to the position of absurdity when the self-contradictory consequences of his own assumptions were revealed. The dialectic was thus a rejection of views by *reductio ad absurdum* argument. Technically this was known as *prasaṅga*.

R. H. Robinson points out in his '*Early Mādhyamika* in India and China' that the stanzas in the Madhyamaka Śāstra of Nāgārjuna contain a large number of hypothetical syllogisms. In the stanzas, there are examples of the two valid types of hypothetical syllogism—modus ponens and modus tollens, and also the fallacious mode in which the antecedent is negated. As an example of 'modus ponens', he cites 3.2. (Prasannapadā); and as an example of 'modus tollens', he cites 19, 6. (Prasannapadā).

He rightly maintains that in the stanzas, there are many dilemmas and the commonest type is of the form; "If *p*, then *q*; if not-*p*, then *q*" which is a special form of the "simple constructive dilemma" of Western Logic.

Another form of dilemma found in the stanzas is: "If *p*, then *q*; if not-*p*, then *r* which is a special form of "Complex constructive dilemma" of Western Logic.

The Purpose of The Dialectic

The purpose of the dialectic was to *disprove* the views advanced by others, not to prove any view of one's own. He who advances a view must necessarily prove it to others whom he wants to convince; he who has no view to advance is under no such necessity. Nāgārjuna states clearly in his *Vigrahavyāvartanī* (St.29) that no one can find fault with the Mādhyamika, for he has no view of his own to advance.

Yadi kācana pratijñā syān me tata eva me bhaved doṣaḥ./
Nāsti ca mama pratijñā tasmān naivāsti me doṣaḥ//

"If I had a thesis of my own to advance, you could find fault with it. Since I have no thesis to advance, the question of disproving it does not arise."

The dialectic was directed against the dogmatists and rationalists who maintained a definite view about Reality. By exposing the hollowness of their logic and the self-contradictory consequences of their assumptions, Nāgārjuna wanted to disprove the claims of Reason to apprehend Reality. Candrakīrti puts the whole position very clearly in the following words:

Nirupapattika-pakṣābhyupagamāt svātmānam eva ayaṁ kevalaṁ visaṁvādayan na śaknoti pareṣāṁ niścayam ādhātum iti. Idameva asya spaṣṭataraṁ dūṣaṇaṁ yaduta svapratijñātārthasādhanāsāmarthyam iti (P.P, p.6) "By his illogical assumption, the opponent only contradicts himself, and is unable to convince others. What could be more self-convicting than the fact that he is unable even to prove the premises on the basis of which he advances his arguments."

Nāgārjuna mercilessly demolished every philosophical opinion of his time, not because he derived a sadistic pleasure in doing so, but because he had a definite purpose. Negatively the dialectic was meant to prove that Reality could not be measured by the three-foot rule of discursive thought. But this was not all. It had some positive suggestions. Firstly, phenomenon or empirical reality is a realm of relativity, in which an entity is *śūnya* or *nis-svabhāva* i.e., devoid of independent reality or unconditionedness.

Secondly, one can comprehend Reality by rising to a plane higher than logical thought i.e., the plane of *prajñā*.

Thirdly, Reality cannot be expressed in terms of the 'is' 'is not'—dichotomising mind.

The Application of the Dialectic

Nāgārjuna rigorously examines all philosophical theories that were held by the thinkers in his time. He turns the battery of his dialectic against concepts like causality, motion and rest, the *āyatanas*, the *skandhas*, the *ātman* etc.

Stcherbatsky has included only his criticism of causality and nirvāṇa, for they are the most important. We shall, therefore, confine our observations only to these two. We shall consider Nāgārjuna's examination of the concept of causality here, and his examination of Nirvāṇa under a separate heading.

Nāgārjuna fires the first shot against causality, for that was the central problem of philosophy in his days.

Examination of Causality

Applying his tetralemma to causality, Nāgārjuna says that there can be only four views about causality, viz. (1) view of *svata utpattiḥ*, the theory of self-becoming (2) *parata utpattiḥ*, i.e. production from another (3) *dvābhyām utpattiḥ* i.e. production from both i.e from itself and from another (4) *ahetuta utpattiḥ* i.e. production without any cause, production by chance.

(1) *Svata utpattiḥ*—This means that the cause and effect are identical, that things are produced out of themselves. Nāgārjuna had evidently in view the Satkāryavāda of Sāṁkhya while criticizing the autogenous theory of causality.

The Mādhyamika's criticism of this theory may be summarized thus:

(i) If the effect is already present in the cause, no purpose would be served by its re-production. The Sāṁkhya may say that though the effect may be present in the cause, its manifestation (*abhivyakti*) is something new. This, however, does not mean that the effect is a new substance. It only means that it is a new form or state of the substance. But this difference of form or state goes against the identity of the underlying substratum.

(ii) If it is said that the cause is partly actual, and partly potential, it would amount to accepting opposed natures in one and the same thing.

If the cause is wholly potential, it cannot by itself become actual without an extraneous aid. The oil cannot be got out of the seed, unless it is pressed by a crusher. If it has to depend on an external aid, then there is no *svata utpattiḥ* or self-production. This amounts to giving up *satkāryavāda*.

(iii) If the cause and effect are identical, it would be impossible to distinguish one as the producer of the other.

The identity view of cause and effect (*Satkāryavāda*) is, therefore, riddled with self-contradiction.

(2) *Parata Utpattiḥ*. This means that the cause and effect are different. This view is known as *asatkāryavāda*. This was held by the Sarvāstivādins and Sautrāntikas or the Hīnayānists in general. Nāgārjuna had obviously these in view while criticizing this heterogeneous view of causality.

His criticism of this view makes out the following important points:

(i) If the cause is different from the effect, no relation can subsist between the two. In that case anything can be produced from anything.

(ii) The Hīnayānist believed that with the production of the effect the cause ceased to exist. But *ex hypothesi* causality is a relation between two. Unless the cause and effect co-exist, they cannot be related. If they cannot be related, causality becomes meaningless.

(iii) The Hīnayānist believed that the effect is produced by a combination of factors. Now for the co-ordination of these factors, another factor would be required, and again for the co-ordination of the additional factor with the previous one, another factor would be required. This would lead to a *regressus ad infinitum.*

(3) *Dvābhyām utpattiḥ*—This theory believes that the effect is both identical with and different from the cause. This is a combination of both Satkāryavāda and Asatkāryavāda, and so contains the inconsistencies of both. Besides this would invest the real with two opposed characters (identity and difference) at one and the same time.

(4) *Ahetutaḥ Utpattiḥ*—This theory maintains that things are produced without a cause, by chance. The Svabhāvavādins—Naturalists and Sceptics believed in such a theory. If no reason is assigned for the theory, it amounts to sheer, perverse dogmatism. If a reason is assigned, it amounts to accepting a cause.

Having exposed the inherent inconsistency in all the above views, Nāgārjuna comes to the conclusion that causality is a mere thought-construct superimposed upon the objective order of existence. In the words of Kant, causality is only a category of mind.

Positive Contribution of Nāgārjuna

From a reading of the Madhyamaka Kārikās, it appears that Nāgārjuna was only an intransigent negativist. In his *Mahāprajñāpāramitā Śāstra,* however, as ably expounded by Dr. K. Venkaṭa Ramanan, Nāgārjuna states his positive views on the vexed question of Reality.

1. Both the *Madhyamaka Kārikā* and the *Mahāprajñā-*

pāramitā Śāstra point to the *naiḥsvābhāvya* or unsubstantiality, conditionedness, relativity as the basic import of *Śūnyatā* with regard to the mundane nature of things, but the *śāstra* brings out more clearly than the *kārikā* the deeper implication of the unsubstantiality of the mundane entities. It says that the tendency of man to seize the relative as the absolute is, at root, the secret-inchoate longing in the heart of man for the absolute (*dharmaiṣaṇā*). Owing to inveterate Ignorance, this longing is misapplied. Man clings to the relative as the absolute only to meet with frustration. But if he clings to the *distinction* of the absolute and the relative as *absolute separateness*, then again he commits the error of 'clinging' in another form. Nāgārjuna is at pains to bring home to man the deeper truth that the unconditioned', the absolute is not only the ground of the conditioned or relative, it is in fact the ultimate nature of the relative itself, and not another entity *apart* from it.

2. The absolute, the unconditioned is not only the ultimate nature of the conditioned mundane entities, it is also the ultimate nature of man. It is because of this that his hunger for the real acquires a deeper significance. As an individual, man is certainly related to the rest of the world, to phenomena, to his *skandhas*, to the contingent, conditioned environment, but he is not alienated from the unconditioned which is the ultimate nature of his very being; he is not bound for ever to his apparent fragmentariness. Being engrossed completely in the passing show of the conditioned entities, and asleep to the inner meaning of his being, he seizes the relative as if it were the absolute and thus invites inevitable suffering. Once he is awake to the conditionedness (Śūnyatā) of the conditioned, his sense of values changes. He becomes a transformed man and then his *dharmaiṣaṇā*, his mysterious longing for the Real finds its meaning and fulfilment. The Kārikā emphasizes the insufficiency, the incompleteness, the unsubstantiality of the *dharmas* (entities) and the *pudgala* (the empirical individual). The Śāstra emphasizes the axiological significance of this sense of incompleteness, and maintains that it is the keen realization of this insufficiency that fans man's tiny spark of longing for the Real, the absolute into the living flame of truth.

3. Practically all the basic concepts of Nāgārjuna's philosophy are found in the Kārikā but then they are over-

shadowed by the overwhelmingly negative character of approach. And it could not be otherwise, for in the Kārikā, Nāgārjuna has all along used the technique of *prasaṅga vākya*, argument of *reductio ad absurdum* character. His main concern is to expose the absurdities involved in accepting what is only relative (niḥsvabhāva) as absolute (sasvabhāva). Even in the Kārikā, Nāgārjuna avers with unmistakable forthrightness that the conditioned bespeaks the unconditioned as its ultimate ground. "That which is of the nature of coming and going, arising and perishing, in its conditioned aspect is itself Nirvāṇa in its unconditioned aspect". (XXV, 9)

Distinction Between Hīnayāna and Mahāyāna

There are several aspects of Buddhist philosophy and religion in which Mahāyāna differs from Hīnayāna. In what follows, we shall deal mostly with the Madhyamaka system of Mahāyāna.

(1) *Difference in the Interpretation of Pratītyasamutpāda*— The doctrine of Pratītyasamutpāda is exceedingly important in Buddhism. It is the causal law both of the universe and the lives of individuals. It is important from two points of view. Firstly, it gives a very clear idea of the impermanent and conditioned nature of all phenomena. Secondly, it shows how birth, old age, death and all the miseries of phenomenal existence arise in dependence upon conditions, and how all the miseries cease in the absence of these conditions.

We have seen what view the Mādhyamikas held of causality. Since Pratītyasamutpāda was the universal causal law, the Mādhyamikas undertook a critical examination of this law. Their interpretation of this law differs considerably from that of Hīnayāna. Pratītyasamutpāda is generally translated as 'conditioned co-production' or 'interdependent origination'.

According to Hīnayāna, *pratītyasamutpāda* means *prati prati ityānāṁ vināśināṁ samutpādaḥ* i.e. "the evanescent momentary things appear." According to it, *pratītya-samutpāda* is the causal law regulating the coming into being and disappearance of the various elements (*dharmas*).

According to the Mādhyamika rise and subsidence of the

elements of existence (*dharmas*) is not the correct interpretation of *pratītyasamutpāda*.

As Candrakīrti puts it *hetupratyayāpekṣo bhāvānām utpādaḥ pratītyasamutpādārthaḥ* (P. P., p. 2) i.e. *pratītyasamutpāda* means the manifestation of entities as relative to causes and conditions.

The Hīnayānists had interpreted *pratītyasamutpāda* as temporal sequence of real entities between which there was a causal relation.

According to the Mādhyamika, *pratītyasamutpāda* does not mean the principle of temporal sequence, but the principle of essential dependence of things on each other. In one word, it is the principle of relativity . Relativity is the most important discovery of modern science. What science has discovered to-day, the great Buddha had discovered two thousand five hundred years before. In interpreting *pratītyasamutpāda* as essential dependence of things on each other or relativity of things, the Mādhyamika means to controvert another doctrine of the Hīnayānist. The Hīnayānists had analysed all phenomena into elements (*dharmas*), and believed that these *dharmas* had a separate reality of their own. The Mādhyamika says that the very doctrine of *pratītyasamutpāda* declares that all the *dharmas* are relative, they have no separate reality (*svabhāva*) of their own. *Nis-svabhāvatva* is synonymous with *śūnyatā* i.e. devoid of real, independent existence. Phenemena are devoid (*śūnya*) of independent reality. *Pratītyasamutpāda* or Inter-dependence means Relativity, and Relativity connotes the unreality (*śūnyatā*) of the separate elements.

Candrakīrti says, *Tadatra-nirodhādyaṣṭa-viśeṣaṇa-viśiṣṭaḥ pratītyasamutpādaḥ śāstrābhidheyārthaḥ* (P. P. P. 2) i.e., "The subject matter or the central idea of this treatise is *pratītya-samutpāda* characterized by eight negative characteristics."

The importance of *pratītyasamutpāda* lies in its teaching that all phenomenal existence, all entities in the world are conditioned, are devoid of (*śūnya*) real, independent existence (*svabhāva*).

As Nāgārjuna puts it *Nahi svabhāvo bhāvānām pratyayādiṣu vidyate* (M. K. 1, 5)—"There is no real, independent existence of entities in the *pratyayas* i.c. conditions". As Dr. E. Conze puts it "All the concrete content belongs to the interplay of countless conditions" (*Buddhist Thought in India*, p. 240).

Nāgārjuna sums up his teaching about *pratītya-samutpāda* in the following words:

Apratītya samutpanno dharmaḥ kaścinna vidyate. Yasmāt tasmāt aśūnyo hi dharmaḥ kaścinna vidyate (M. K, 24, 19) "Since there is no element of existence (*dharma*) which comes into manifestation without conditions, therefore there is no *dharma* which is not *śūnya* (devoid of real independent existence)."

The *pratītyasamutpāda* becomes equivalent to *śūnyatā* or relativity. Nāgārjuna says *Yaḥ pratītyasamutpādaḥ śūnyatāṁ tām pracakṣmahe.* (M. K. 24, 18) "What is *pratītyasamutpāda* that we call *śūnyatā*".

Śūnya or *śūnyatā* is the most important concept of Madhyamaka philosophy. We shall, therefore, consider it under a separate heading in the sequel.

In the Kārikā, however, the main purpose of Nāgārjuna was to clear the ground for the exposition of his positive philosophy, viz., the role of *prajñā* in comprehending the different levels of understanding. He gives a detailed exposition of *prajñā* in the śāstra. Again in the Kārikā there is no direct reference to *dharmaiṣaṇā*, the secret longing for the Real imbedded in the human heart. In the Śāstra, this *dharmaiṣaṇā* becomes the burden of his song. In the Kārikā, there is hardly any description of the course of wayfaring towards the goal; in the Śāstra this is vividly described. In the Kārikā, the unconditioned as the immanent reality of the conditioned is only obliquely hinted at; in the Śāstra, it receives prominent attention. The chapter on *tathatā* particularly brings to light the immanence of the real in every being. The chapter on *bhūtakoṭi* gives an illuminating description of *upāya*, the skilfulness of non-clinging. Thus the Śāstra is complementary to the kārikā.

2. *Difference in the concept of Nirvāṇa*

The following points regarding Nirvāṇa are common between Hīnayāna and Mahāyāna.

(1) Nirvāṇa is inexpressible. It has no origin, no change, no decay. It is deathless (*amṛta*).

(2) It has to be realized within oneself. This is possible only when there is complete extinction of craving for sense-pleasure.

(3) Personal self as such ceases in Nirvāṇa. Access to Nirvāṇa is possible only on the extinction of the personal self.

(4) It is a peace (*śama* or *upaśama*) that passeth understanding.

(5) It provides lasting security.

The word 'nirvāṇa' literally means extinguished' and therefore 'tranquil'.

There are four ways in which Nirvāṇa is generally described in Buddhist literature; viz., (1) negative, (2) positive, (3) paradoxical and (4) symbolic.

1. Negative—The negative description is the most common. Nirvāṇa is (1) *amṛta* (deathless), (2) unchanging, (3) imperishable (*acyuta*), (4) without end (*ananta*), (5) non-production, (6) extinction of birth, (7) unborn, (8) not liable to dissolution (*apalokina*), (9) uncreated (*abhūtam*), (10) free from disease, (11) unaging, (12) freedom from transmigration, (13) *anuttaram* (utmost), (14) cessation of pain (*duḥkha-nirodha*), (15) final release (*apavagga*).

2. Positive : Nirvāṇa is (1) peace (*śama or upaśama*); The following verse of *Mahāparinirvāṇasūtra* brings out this idea very clearly:

anityā vata saṁskārā utpāda-vyaya-dharmiṇaḥ |
utpadya hi nirudhyante teṣām vyapaśamas sukham ||

"Impermanent, indeed, are all conditioned things. It is their very nature to come into being and then to cease. Having been produced, they are stopped. Their cessation brings peace and ease."

Śama or *upaśama* connotes extinction of craving, cessation of suffering and a state of calm.

(2) bliss—*Nibbānam paramaṁ sukham*
"Nirvāṇa is the supreme bliss."

(3) *Sambodhi or prajñā* (transcendental wisdom)

(4) *jñāna* (illumination) or *viññāṇam*—pure, radiant consciousness.

(5) security (*kṣamam*)

3. Paradoxical. This statement is mostly found in Prajñāpāramitā or Mahāyānika literature. Nirvāṇa is abiding in a state of non-abiding. The only way of reaching the goal is to

realize that in the ultimate sense there is no goal to be reached. Nirvāṇa is reality which is *śūnya* (void).

4. Symbolical: Symbolical description differs from the paradoxical in avoiding to speak in abstractions and using concrete images instead. From this standpoint, Nirvāṇa is (1) the cool cave, (2) the island in the floods, (3) the further shore, (4) the holy city, (5) the refuge, (6) the shelter, (7) the asylum.

A question that arises in this connexion is whether Nirvāṇa is only a transformed state of the mind or whether it is another dimension of being. The word has been used both for a transformed psychological state and for a metaphysical status.

Buddhist literature is full of statements which go to show that Nirvāṇa is a transformed state of personality and consciousness. The transformation is described in negative terms as the destruction of *taṇhā* (craving) and *āsavas* (obsessions) and in positive terms as the emergence of *prajñā* or *sambodhi* (transcendental wisdom) and *Śānti* (peace).

While the emphasis is on the transformed psychological state, there are also statements which go to show that Nirvāṇa has a metaphysical status, that it is a different dimension of being.

Two quotations will suffice.

The Buddha is said to have made the following remark about Nirvāṇa:

"There is an Unborn, Unbecome, Unmade, Uncompounded; for if there were not this Unborn, Unbecome, Unmade, Uncompounded, there would be apparently no escape from this here that is born, become, made, and compounded" (*Udāna*, VIII.3)

This goes to show that Nirvāṇa is not annihilation, that the aspirant enters a different dimension of being. Some have tried to explain it away as a mere transformed state of personality. The logic of the words does not permit such an interpretation. There is, however, another statement in Udāna which cannot, by any linguistic *tour de force* be interpreted as mere transformation of personality. It is as follows:

Atthi bhikkhave tad āyatanaṁ, yattha n 'eva paṭhavī na āpo/na tejo va vāyo na ākāsānañcāyatanam, viññāṇāñcāyatanaṁ na ākiñcaññāyatanaṁ na nevasaññānāsaññānāññāyatanaṃ nāyaṁ loko na paraloko ubho candimasūriyā, tad aham bhikkhave n'eva āgatiṁ vadāmi na gatiṁ, na ṭhitiṁ na cutiṁ na upapattim appatiṭṭhaṁ appatiṭṭhaṁ-appavattaṁ anārammaṇaṁ eva taṁ, eś ev' anto dukkhassā' ti (*Udāna*, 80). "There is that sphere wherein is neither earth nor water nor fire nor air; wherein is neither the sphere of infinite space nor of infinite consciousness nor of nothingness/nor of neither-ideation—nor, non-ideation; where there is neither this world nor a world beyond nor both together nor moon nor sun: I say there is neither coming from it nor going to it; it has neither duration nor decay; there is neither beginning nor establishment; there is no result and no cause; this verily is the end of suffering."

This long quotation leaves no room for doubt that it refers to Nirvāṇa as a different dimension of being. Actually however, Nirvāṇa is ineffable.

In *Saṁyutta Nikāya* (1069-76),there is a long dialogue between Upaśiva and Buddha about Nirvāṇa. In that dialogue, the following two statements made by the Buddha are very significant:

Accī yathā vātavegena khitto
atthaṁ paleti, na upeti saṅkhaṁ/
evam munī nāmakāyā vimutto
atthaṁ paleti, na upeti saṅkhaṁ.//

"As flame blown out by wind goes to rest, and is lost to cognizance, just so the sage who is released from name and body, goes to rest and is lost to cognizance".

Atthaṅ-gatassa na pamāṇaṁ atthi;
yena naṁ vajju, taṁ tassa n'atthi;
sabbesu dhammesu samūhatesu
samūhatā vādapathā pi sabbeti.

"There is no measure to him who has gone to rest; he keeps nothing that could be named. When all *dharmas* are abolished, all paths of speech are also abolished." (Conze's translation)

Both Hīnayānists and Mahāyānists would concur in these beautiful descriptions of Nirvāṇa. It is only on the stepping-stone of our dead selves that we can rise to Nirvāṇa. As Suzuki puts it "Nirvāṇa according to Buddhists, does not signify an annihilation of consciousness nor a temporary or permanent suppression of mentation, as imagined by some but it is the annihilation of the notion of ego-substance and of all the desires that arise from this erroneous conception." (*Outlines of Mahāyāna Buddhism*, pp. 50-51)

We shall now turn to the difference in the interpretation of Nirvāṇa between the two.

(1) The Hīnayānists believe that Nirvāṇa is eternal (*nitya*), blissful (*sukha*).

The Mādhyamika says that there can be no predication of Nirvāṇa.

(2) Hīnayānists believe that it is something to be acquired. Mādhyamikas believe that it is not something to be acquired.

Nāgārjuna describes Nirvāṇa in the following words:

Aprahīṇaṁ asamprāptaṁ anucchinnaṁ aśāśvataṁ/
Aniruddhaṁ anutpannaṁ etan nirvāṇaṁ ūcyate.//

(M.K. XXV,3)

"Nirvāṇa is that which is neither abandoned nor acquired, it is neither a thing annihilated, nor a thing eternal; it is neither destroyed nor produced."

To quote Candrakīrti *Sarvaprapañcopaśamaśivalakṣaṇaṁ nirvāṇam* (P. P. p. 2). Nirvāṇa connotes the cessation of all talk about it, the quiescence of phenomenal existence, and the attainment of the highest good."

3. The Vaibhāṣika thinks that Nirvāṇa is a positive entity (*bhāva*). Nāgārjuna says that the Hīnayānist believes Nirvāṇa to be unconditioned. To say it is unconditioned (*asaṁskṛta*), and yet a positive entity (*bhāva*) amounts to self-contradiction, for a positive entity which is not dependent on conditions cannot be discovered. If it is not *bhāva*, it cannot be *abhāva* (total cessation) either, for *abhāva* is a relative word. There can be *abhāva* only when previously there is *bhāva*. Moreover cessation (*abhāva*) is an event, occurring in time. It would make Nirvāṇa transitory.

Candrakīrti in his commentary on *Madhyamaka Kārikā* gives a relevant quotation from *Ārya Ratnāvalī*.

Na cābhāvo' pi nirvāṇam kuta evāsya bhāvanā /
Bhāvābhāvaparāmarśa-kṣayo nirvāṅam ucyate. //

(P.P., p. 229)

"Nor is Nirvāṇa abhāva (non-ens). How do you entertain such an idea? Nirvāṇa is really complete cessation of such consideration as *bhāva* (ens) or *abhāva* (non-ens) of the real." It is above the relativity of existence and non-existence. Candrakīrti clinches the whole issue by saying *Tataśca sarvakalpanā-kṣayarūpam eva nirvāṇam* (P., P. p. 229) Nirvāṇa or Reality is that which is absolved of all thought - constructs.

4. The Hīnayānist thinks that *Nirvāṇa* is the opposite of *saṁsāra* (phenomena). Nāgārjuna says that there is no difference between *Nirvāṇa* and *saṁsāra.*

Na saṁsārasya nirvāṇāt kiñcid asti viśeṣaṇaṃ |
Na nirvāṇasya saṁsārāt kiñcid asti viśeṣaṇaṃ. ||

(M.K. XXV, 19)

"Nothing of phenomenal existence (*saṁsāra*) is different from *nirvāṇa*, nothing of *nirvāṇa* is different from phenomenal existence."

Nirvāṇasya ca yā koṭiḥ koṭiḥ saṁsaraṇasya ca |
Na tayor antaraṁ kiñcit susūkṣmam api vidyate ||

(M.K. XXV, 20)

"That which is the limit of Nirvāṇa is also the limit of *saṁsāra*; there is not the slightest difference between the two"

Ya ājavaṁjavībhāva upādāya pratītya vā|
So' pratītya anupādāya nirvāṇam upadiśyate||

(MK., XXV, 9)

"That which when appropriating or relative (*upādāya*) or dependent (*pratitya vā*) wanders to and fro (*ājavaṁjavībhāva*) in its conditioned nature is declared to be Nirvāṇa when not depending (*apratītya*) or not appropriating or relative (*anupādāya*) i.e., in its unconditioned nature.

To sum up, there are two main features which distinguish the Mādhyamika conception of Nirvāṇa from that of the Hīnayānist.

(1) The Hīnayānist considers certain defiled and conditioned *dharmas* (elements) to be ultimately real, and also certain undefiled and unconditioned *dharmas* to be ultimately real. According to him, Nirvāṇa means a veritable change of the discrete, conditioned existences (*saṁskṛta dharmas*) and defilements ((*kleśas*) into unconditioned (*asaṁskṛta*) and undefiled *dharmas*. The Mādhyamika says that Nirvāṇa does not mean a change in the objective order, the change is only subjective. It is not the world that we have to change, but only ourselves. If the *kleśas* (defilements) and the *saṁskṛta dharmas* (conditioned existences) were ultimately real, no power on earth could

change them. The change is in our outlook; it is a psychological transformation, not an ontological one. Suzuki sums up the Mādhyamika position about Nirvāṇa in the following words: "Theoretically, Nirvāṇa is the dispersion of the clouds hovering round the light of Bodhi. Morally, it is the suppression of egoism and the awakening of love (*karuṇā*). Religiously it is the absolute surrender of the self to the will of the Dharmakāya." (*Outlines of M. Buddhism*, p. 369). It may be added that ontologically it is the Absolute itself. "Nirvāṇa is not something which can be abandoned or acquired, neither a thing annihilated nor a thing eternal; it is neither destroyed nor produced." (M.K., XXV, 3). No change can be effected in the Absolute or Reality. It is as it has always been. A change has to be effected only in ourselves.

2. The Absolute and the Empirical, the Noumenon and the Phenomena, Nirvāṇa and Saṁsāra are not two sets of separate realities set over against each other. The Absolute or Nirvāṇa viewed through the thought-constructs (*vikalpa*) is saṁsāra, the world or *saṁsāra* viewed *sub specie aeternitatis* is the Absolute or Nirvāṇa itself.

It may be said in passing that much of the confusion regarding Nirvāṇa is due to the fact that the same word Nirvāṇa is used for the psychological change consequent on the extinction of craving and the sense of ego, and also for the ontological Reality or the Absolute. It should be borne in mind that Nāgārjuna is using the word Nirvāṇa throughout the twenty-fifth chapter of the *Madhyamaka Karikā* in the sense of the Absolute Reality and it is from this standpoint that his criticism has been levelled against the Hīnayānist.

3. *Difference in Ideal*

The ideal of Hīnayāna is Arhatship or Arhantship; the ideal of Mahāyāna is that of the Bodhisattva. To put it in simple English, the ideal of Hīnayāna is individual enlightenment; the ideal cf Mahāyāna is universal enlightenment.

The word 'yāna' is generally translated as way, path or vehicle. In his "Survey of Buddhism", Bhikshu Saṅgharakṣita suggests 'career' for 'yāna'. This seems to be the best English equivalent for 'yāna'.

There were three *yānas* known to Early Buddhism, viz., Śrāvaka-yāna, Pratyekabuddha-yāna and Bodhisattva-yāna.

Śrāvaka (Pāli-*Sāvaka*) literally means 'hearer'. This name was given to the disciple who having heard i.e, learned the truth from the Buddha or any of his disciples aims at Arhantship. Arhat or Arhant means the status of the holy man who has won enlightenment. The word 'Arhat' means etymologically 'worthy'. Another meaning that is suggested in some Buddhist books is 'one who has slain (*han*) the enemies (*ari*) i. e. the kleśas or defilements'.

Pratyekabuddha (Pāli, *Paccekabuddha*) is one who in 'solitary singleness', in independence of all external support, attains Arhatship. The word 'pratyeka' means 'private', 'individual', 'single', 'solitary'. He does not share with others his hard-won knowledge of the means for the attainment of Nirvāṇa. He believes that others too, driven by the stern reality of the miseries of life, may some day take to the holy path, but does not bother to teach or enlighten them.

The above two adepts represent the ideal of individualism. They consider enlightenment as an individual not a social or cosmic achievement.

The Bodhisattva (Pāli, *Boddhisatta*) seeks supreme enlightenment not for himself alone but for all sentient beings. Bodhisattvayāna has for its aim the attainment of Supreme Buddhahood. It is, therefore, also called the Buddhayāna or Tathāgatayāna. The word 'bodhi' means 'perfect wisdom,' or better 'transcendental wisdom', supreme enlightenment. The word 'sattva' means 'essence.' The word 'bodhi' is untranslatable. It is the reflex of the consciousness of Dharmakāya in human beings. A Bodhisattva is one who has the essence or potentiality of transcendental wisdom or supreme enlightenment, who is on the way to the attainment of transcendental wisdom. He is a potential Buddha. His career lasts for aeons of births in each of which he prepares himself for final Buddhahood by the practice of the six perfections and the stages of moral and spiritual discipline (*daśabhūmi*) and lives a life of heroic struggle and unremitting self-sacrifice for the good of all sentient creatures.

Boddhisattva has in him *bodhi-citta* and *praṇidhānabala.* There are two aspects of *bodhi-citta*, viz. *prajñā* (transcendental wisdom) and *Karuṇā* (universal love). *Praṇidhānabala* is the inflexible resolve to save all sentient creatures. These are the three aspects of Dharmakāya (the Absolute Personalized) as reflected in the religious consciousness of Bodhisattva. Prajñā is the highest expression of the cognitive side; *karuṇā* is the highest expression of the emotive side, and *praṇidhānabala* is the highest expression of the volitional side of consciousness. Bodhisattva thus develops all the aspects of consciousness.

Bodhicitta is the most important characteristic of Bodhisattva. On the basis of Nāgārjuna's 'Discourse on the Transcendentality of the Bodhicitta, Suzuki gives a detailed description of *bodhicitta* in his *Outlines of Mahāyāna Buddhism.* It may be summarized thus:

(1) The *bodhicitta* is free from all determinations—the five *skandhas*, the twelve *āyatanas* and the eighteen *dhātus*. It is not particular, but universal.

(2) Love is the essence of the Bodhicitta, therefore, all Bodhisattvas find their *raison d' etre* in this.

(3) The *bodhicitta* abiding in the heart of sameness (*samatā*) creates individual means of salvation (*upāya*).

The Bodhisattva has to pass through ten stages of development (*daśa bhūmis*), viz. (1) *pramuditā* (delight)—which he feels in passing from the narrow ideal of personal Nirvāṇa to the higher ideal of emancipating all sentient creatures from the thraldom of ignorance, (2) *vimalā*—negatively 'freedom from defilement', positively 'purity of heart', (3) *prabhākarī*—the penetrating insight into the impermanence of all things, (4) *arciṣmatī*—In this the Bodhisattva practises passionlessness and detachment and burns the twin coverings (*āvaraṇas*) of defilement and ignorance (5) *sudurjayā*—In this he develops *samatā*—the spirit of sameness, and enlightenment by means of meditation. (6) *abhimukhī* or Face to Face.—In this the Bodhisattva stands face to face with Reality. He realizes the sameness of all phenomena, (7) *dūraṅgamā* or the far-going.—In this he acquires the knowledge that enables him to adopt any means for his work of salvation. He has won Nirvāṇa, but without entering it, he is busily engaged for the emancipation of all, (8) *acalā* or the immovable.—In this, the Bodhisattva experiences the *anutpattika-dharma-kṣānti* or acquiescence in the unoriginatedness of all phenomena. He knows in detail the evolution and involution of the universe. (9) *Sādhumatī*—In this he acquires comprehensive knowledge, unfathomable by ordinary human intelligence. He knows the desires and thoughts of men and is able to teach them according to their capacities, (10) *dharmameghā*. In this he acquires perfection of contemplation, knows the mystery of existence, and is consecrated as perfect. He attains Buddhahood.

The ideal of Hīnayāna was Arhatship or attainment of personal enlightenment. The ideal of Mahāyāna was Bodhisattvayāna. Śrāvakayāna and Pratyekabuddhayāna, according to Mahāyāna aimed at mere individual enlightenment which was a narrow ideal. Bodhisattvayāna aimed at universal enlightenment. It was the destiny of every individual to become a Buddha. The Bodhisattva ideal of Mahāyāna was higher (*mahā*); that of Hīnayāna was inferior (*hīna*).

The difference in the spiritual ideal of the two is expressed in yet another way. The ideal of Hīnayāna is Nirvāṇa; the ideal of Mahāyāna is Buddhatva, the attainment of Buddhahood. The Mahāyānist does not consider the attainment of Nirvāṇa to be the highest ideal, but the attainment of Buddhatva i.e. *prajñā* (transcendental insight) and *karuṇā* (universal love) to be the highest ideal.

4. *Difference regarding the means for the attainment of Nirvāṇa*

The Hīnayānist believes that by the realization of *pudgala-nairātmya* (not-self or unsubstantiality of the person), one could attain Nirvāṇa.

The Mahāyānist maintains that it is not only by the realization of *pudgala-nairātmya*, but also by the realization of *dharma-nairātmya* (i.e. that all the *dharmas* or elements of existence are unsubstantial, devoid of any independent reality of their own) that one really attains Nirvāṇa.

According to Mahāyāna , the realization of both *pudgala nairātmya* and *dharma-nairātmya* is necessary for the attainment of Nirvāṇa.

5. *Difference regarding the removal of the āvaraṇas or obstacles*

Closely connected with the above is the question of the removal of the *āvaraṇas*.

The Hīnayānist says that man is unable to attain Nirvāṇa, because Reality is hidden by the veil (*āvaraṇa*) of passions like attachment, aversion, delusion (*kleśāvaraṇa*). The *kleśāvaraṇa* acts as an obstacle in the way of the realization of Nirvāṇa. The *kleśāvaraṇa* has, therefore, to be removed before one can attain Nirvāṇa. The *kleśas*, however, depend for their activity on the belief of an identical personal self (*satkāyadṛṣṭi*). It is only by realizing *pudgala-nairātmya* i.e. the non-reality or unsubstantiality of a personal self that the *kleśas* or the obstacles can be removed, and only when the *kleśas* are removed can Nirvāṇa be attained. The removal of *Kleśāvaraṇa* is thus connected with the realization of *pudgala-nairātmya*, The Hīnayānist considers the removal of *kleśāvaraṇa* alone as sufficient for the attainment of Nirvāṇa.

The Mahāyānist says that Reality is veiled not only by *kleśāvaraṇa* but also by *jñeyāvaraṇa* or the veil that hides true knowledge. The removal, therefore, of *jñeyāvaraṇa* is also necessary. This is possible by the realization of *dharmanairātmya* or *dharmaśūnyatā*, the egolessness and emptiness of all elements of existence.

Just as the removal of *kleśāvaraṇa* is connected with the realization of *pudgala-nairātmya*, so the removal of *jñeyāvaraṇa* is connected with the realization of *dharmanairātmya*.

The Mahāyānist maintains that the removal of *kleśāvaraṇa* alone is not sufficient for the attainment of full freedom; the removal of *jñeyāvaraṇa* is also necessary.

6. *Difference in the Concept of Dharma*

The Hīnayānists believed in certain ultimate reals, called *dharmas*. The word *dharma* in this sense is difficult to translate. It is sometimes translated as 'things'. It should be borne in mind that *dharmas* are not 'things' in the sense of the crude data of common sense. 'Elements of existence', 'ultimate reals'—these are better translations of *dharmas*. Hīnayāna believes that the world is composed of an unceasing flow of certain *ultimate dharmas* which are simple, momentary and impersonal. Most of them are *Saṁskṛta* (*dharmas* with signs), and some are *asaṁskṛta* (dharmas without signs).

According to Mahāyāna, these *dharmas* are not ultimate realities at all, but only mental constructs. Mahāyāna pointed out that even the so-called ultimate *saṁskṛta* and *asaṁskṛta* dharmas are dependent upon conditions and so relative. Being relative, they are *śūnya* (devoid of reality).

7. *Difference in the concept of Buddhology*

The *rūpa-kāya* of the Buddha was simply the visible physical body. Neither Hīnayāna nor Mahāyāna accepted this as the real Buddha.

Earlier Buddhism had also developed the idea of *nirmāṇa-kāya* which was a fictitious body which the Buddha could assume by his yogic power whenever he liked and by means of which he could appear anywhere. There is no difference of view regarding this body also between the Hīnayānist and the Mādhyamika.

The difference lies in the concept of the *dharma-kāya* of the Buddha. The highest conception regarding the *dharma-kāya* reached by Hīnayāna was that it was the sum total of the qualities (*dharmas*) of the Buddha. When a follower takes refuge in the Buddha it is in this Buddha-nature that he takes refuge. He does not take refuge in Gautama Buddha who is dead and gone.

The Mādhyamika developed the concept of *dharmakāya* in a different way.

The concept of *sambhoga-kāya* was the contribution of the Yogācārins. We shall study the concept of these *kāyas* under a separate heading.

8. *Hīnayāna was intellectual, Mahāyāna devotional also*

Hīnayāna was entirely intellectual. The main concern of the Hīnayānist was to follow the eight-fold path chalked out by the Buddha. In Hīnayāna, it was the human aspect of the Buddha which was emphasized.

In Mahāyāna, Buddha was taken as God, as Supreme Reality itself that had descended on the earth in human form for the good of mankind. The concept of God in Buddhism was never as a creator but as Divine Love that out of compassion embodied itself in human form to uplift suffering humanity. He was worshipped with fervent devotion. The devotion of the Mahāyānist gave rise to the art of sculpture and painting. Beautiful statues of the Buddha were carved out, and excellent imaginative pictures representing him and the various aspects of his life were painted. Mahāyāna maintained that the arduous path of *prajñā* (transcendental wisdom) was meant only for the advanced few, for the average man it was devotion to the Buddha which would enable him to attain Nirvāṇa. Buddha was worshipped in the form of Avalokiteśvara, Amitābha and the future Buddha, Maitreya.

9. *Hīnayīna pluralistic, Mahāyāna non-dualistic*

The philosophy of Hīnayāna was one of radical pluralism, that of Mahāyāna was undiluted non-dualism (advaya).

10. *Hīnayāna rationalistic, Mahāyāna mystic*

The approach to truth adopted by Hīnayāna was one of mystically-tinged rationalism, that adopted by Mahāyāna was one of super-rationalism and profound mysticism.

Main Features of Madhyamaka Philosophy

(1) *Śūnya-Śūnyatā*

The most striking feature of Madhyamaka philosophy is its ever-recurring use of *śūnya* and *śūnyatā*. So central is this idea to the system that it is generally known as *Śūnyavāda* i.e., the philosophy that asserts *Śūnya* as the characterization of Reality.

Śūnya is a most perplexing word in Buddhist philosophy. Non-Buddhists have interpreted it only as nihilism. But that is not what it means.

Etymologically it is derived from the root *śvī* which means 'to swell, to expand'. Curiously enough, the word Brahman is derived from the root 'bṛh' or 'bṛṁh' which also means 'to swell to expand'. The Buddha is said to be seated in *Śūnya tattva,* in the *śūnya* principle'. The word *śūnya* seems to have been used in an ontological sense in such contexts. The implication of the etymological signification of the word does not seem to have been fully worked out.

According to some scholars the word *śūnya* has no ontological signification. It has only a soteriological suggestion. But the word *śūnya* has obviously been used also in an ontological sense with an axiological overtone and soteriological background.

In the ontological sense *śūnya* is the void which is also fulness. Because it is nothing in particular, it has the possibility of every thing. It has been identified with Nirvāṇa., with the Absolute, with Paramārtha-sat (the Supreme Reality), with Tattva (Reality). What is the *śūnya-tattva*? This is what Nāgārjuna has to say:

Aparapratyayaṁ śāntam prapañcair aprapañcitam/
Nirvikalpam anānārtham etattattvasya lakṣaṇam//
(M. K., XVIII, 9)

(1) It is *aparapratyayam.* It is that experience which cannot be imparted to any one by another. It has to be realized by every one for himself.

(2) It is *śāntam* . It is quiescent, unaffected by the empirical mind.

(3) It is *prapañcair aprapañcitam* i.e. inexpressible by the verbalising mind. It is non-determinate.

(4) It is *nirvikalpam* i.e. it is transcendent to discursive thought.

(5) It is *anānārtham.* It is non-dual.

Śūnyatā is an abstract noun derived from *śūnya.* It means deprivation and suggests fulfilment.

The words *Śūnya* and *Śūnyatā* will best be undersood in connexion with *svabhāva. Svabhāva* literally means'own being'. Candrakīrti says that this word has been used in Buddhist philosophy in two ways :

1. The essence or special property of a thing, e.g., 'heat is the *svabhāva* or special property of fire'. *Iha yo dharmo yam padārthaṁ na vyabhicarati, sa tasya svabhāva iti vyapadiśyate, aparāpratibaddhatvāt*" i.e. "In this world an attribute which always accompanies an object, never parts from it, that, not being indissolubly connected with any thing else, is known as the *svabhāva* i. e., special property of that object" (P.P. 105)

2. *Svabhāva* (own-being) as the contrary of *parabhāva* (other-being). Candrakīrti says, *svo bhāvaḥ svabhāva iti yasya padārthasya yadātmīyaṁ rūpaṁ tat tasya svabhāva iti* (P. P. p. 115) "*Svabhāva* is the own being, the very nature of a thing". Nāgārjuna says *akṛtrimaḥ svabhāvo hi nirapekṣaḥ paratra ca* (M. K. 15, 2). "That is really *svabhāva* which is not brought about by anything else, unproduced (*akṛitrimaḥ*), that which is not dependent on, not relative to any thing other than itself, non-contingent, unconditioned (*nirapekṣaḥ paratra ca*)".

The Mādhyamika rejects the first meaning of *svabhāva* and accepts only the second. Candrakīrti says clearly *kṛtrimasya parasāpekṣasya ca svabhāvatvaṁ neṣṭam.* "We do not accept that as *svabhāva* which is brought about by, contingent on, relative to something else". The first sense is not acceptable, for even the so-called *svabhāva* or essential property of a thing is *kṛtrima* and *sāpekṣa,* contingent and relative. Even the heat which is the special property of fire depends on so many conditions—a match, or a lens, fuel, or the friction of two pieces of wood. It is, therefore, not *svabhāva* in the highest sense of the word. In one word *svabhāva* is the Absolute reality, whereas everything else, all phenomena are *parabhāva* (relative).

The word *Śūnya* has to be understood from two points of view, viz. (1) from the point of view of phenomena or empirical reality, it means *svabhāva-śūnya* i.e. *devoid of svabhāva* or independent, substantial reality of its own; (2) from the point of view of the Absolute, it means *prapañca-śūnya* i.e. devoid of *prapañca* or verbalisation, thought-construct and plurality.

(i) We shall consider the word *Śūnya* in its first signification at first. We have discussed the word *svabhāva* at length so that we may be able to understand clearly the word *śūnya* when used in connexion with phenomenal reality or with *dharmas* (elements of existence). In this context *śūnya* invariably means *svabhāva-śūnya,* i.e. empty or devoid of independent, substantial reality. There is not a single thing in the world which is unconditionally, absolutely real. Everything is related to, contingent upon, conditioned by something else. The long discussion of causality or *pratītya-samutpāda* in Madhyamaka Śāstra is only meant to show that not a single thing in the world exists in its own right, nothing has an independent reality of its own. Everything is conditioned by something (*pratītyasamutpanna*). The world is not Reality : it is a realm of relativity. That is why Nāgārjuna says *yaḥ pratītyasamutpādaḥ śūnyatāṁ tām pracakṣmahe.* "There is no real production : there is only manifestation of a thing contingent on causes and conditions. It is this conditioned co-production that we designate as Śūnyatā." There is no real causal relation between entities; there is only *mutual dependence* between entities which means in other words that entities are devoid of independent self-hood (*svabhāva*). Causal relation, therefore, does not mean a sequence of realities but only a *sequence of appearances*. Every thing in the world is dependent upon the sum-total of its conditions. Things are merely appearances. Hence *pratītya-samutpāda* is equated with *śūnyatā* or relativity. The world is not a conglomeration of things. It is simply process, and things are simply events. A 'thing' *by itself* is 'nothing' at all. This is what is meant by the *śūnyatā* or emptiness of all *dharmas*.

(ii) Now let us see what *Śūnyatā* means from the standpoint of the Absolute. From the standpoint of the Absolute, *śūnyatā* means *prapañcair aprapañcitam* that which is devoid of, completely free of thought-construct, *anānārthām*, that which is devoid of plurality. In other words, *śūnyatā* as applied to *tattva* signifies that it is,

(*a*) in-expressible in human language.

(*b*) that 'is', 'not is', 'both is' and 'not is', 'neither is' nor 'not is'—no thought-category or predicate can be applied to it. It is transcendent to thought.

(*c*) that it is free of plurality, that it is a Whole which cannot be sundered into parts.

To sum up, the import of *śūnyatā* may be understood in six ways. Three of these are given together in 18th verse of Chapter XXIV of the Kārikā :

yaḥ pratītyasamutpādaḥ śūnyatāṁ tām pracakṣmahe|
Sā prajñaptirupādāyā pratipat saiva madhyamā||

"That we call *śūnyatā* which is *pratītyasamutpāda, upādāya prajñapti, madhyamā pratipat.*"

1. In reference to *vyavahāra* or empirical reality, *śūnyatā* means *naiḥsvābhāvya* i.e., devoidness of self-being, of unconditioned nature. In other words, it connotes conditiond co-production or *pratītyasamutpāda*—thorough-going relativity.

2. This idea is conveyed in another way by the term, *upādāyaprajñapti* or "derived name" which means that the presence of a name does not mean the reality of the named. Candrakīrti says, *cakrādīnyupādāya rathāṅgāni rathaḥ prajñāpyate* i.e., a chariot is so named by taking into account its parts like wheel etc; it does not mean that the chariot is something different in its own right *apart* from its constituent parts. This is another instance of relativity.

As relativity, *śūnyatā* also connotes the relative, non-absolute nature of specific views.

3. Śūnyatā exposes the folly of accepting any absolute beginning or total cessation and thus connotes *madhyamā pratipat*—taking things as they are and avoiding the extremes (1) is and (2) is not.

Over and above these three, there are other senses in which the word *śūnyatā* has been used in Madhyamaka philosophy.

4. In reference to *paramārtha* or ultimate reality, *śūnyatā* connotes the non-conceptual nature of the absolute.

5. In reference to the aspirant, *śnūyatā* implies his attitude of *anupalambha* or the skilfulness of non-clinging to the relative as the absolute or to the absolute as something specific.

6. The Mahāprajñā-pāramitā Śāstra brings out another implication of the *śūnyatā* principle, viz; *dharmaiṣaṇā*, the irrepressible longing for the Real, beyond the passing show of mundane life.

Axiological significance of Śūnyatā

Śūnyatā is not merely a word of ontological signification. It has also an axiological implication. Since all empirical things are devoid of substantial reality, therefore they are 'worthless'. It is because of our ignorance that we attach so much value to worldly things. Once *Śūnyatā* is properly understood, the inordinate craving for the mad rush after a thing that :

> 'Like snow upon the Desert's dusty face
> Lighting a little hour or two is gone'

ceases, and we experience the blessing of peace.

Soteriological significance of Śūnyatā

Śūnyatā is not merely an intellectual concept. Its realization is a means in salvation. When rightly grasped, it leads to the negation of the multiplicity of the *dharmas* and to detachment from the 'passing show' of the tempting things of life. Meditation on *Śūnyatā* leads to *prajñā* (transcendental wisdom) which brings about the emancipation of the aspirant from spiritual darkness. Nāgārjuna puts the quintessence of his teachings about *Śūnyatā* in the following verse:

Karmakleśa-kṣayānmokṣaḥ karmakleśā vikalpataḥ//
Te prapañcāt prapañcastu śūnyatāyāṁ nirudhyate//

(M. K. xviii, 5)

"Emancipation is obtained by the dissolution of selfish deeds and passions All selfish deeds and passions are caused by imaginative constructs which value worthless things as full of worth. The *vikalpas* or imaginative constructs are born of *prapañca*, the verbalizing, imaging activity of the mind. This activity of the mind ceases when *Śūnyatā*, emptiness or hollowness of things is realized."

Śūnya as the symbol of the inexpressible

Śūnya is used in Madhyamaka philosophy as a symbol of the inexpressible. In calling Reality *śūnya*, the Mādhyamika only means to say that it is *avācya, anabhilāpya* i.e., inexpressible. In the very first verse of *Madhyamaka Kārika*, Nāgārjuna makes the standpoint of *Śūnyavāda* luminously prominent. The standpoint consists of the eight 'Nos'.

Anirodham anutpādam anucchedam aśāśvatam/
Anekārtham anānārtham anāgamam anirgamam.//

It is (1) *anirodham*, beyond destruction, (2) *anutpādam*, beyond production, (3) *anucchedam*, beyond dissolution, (4) *aśāśvatam*, beyond eternity. (5) *anekārtham*—beyond oneness, (6) *anānārtham*—beyond plurality, (7) *anāgamam* beyond ingress (8) *anirgamam*—beyond egress.

In short, Reality is beyond the dichotomies of the intellect. It in inexpressible. The word 'śūnya' (or śūnyatā) has been used in this system, now and then, as indicative of *avācya, avyākṛta*.

Śūnyatā not a theory

We have seen that the Mādhyamika uses the dialectic as a criticism of all *dṛṣṭis* (theories) without any theory of his own. By the use of his dialectic, he reaches the conclusion that all the *dharmas* are *śūnya* or *nissvabhāva* i.e. devoid of any independent, substantial reality.

It may be thought that *śūnyatā* itself is a theory. But this would be a misreading of the Mādhyamika's position. *Śūnyatā* is not a theory. It is at once the awareness of the impotence of Reason to realize Truth and the urge to rise to a level higher than Reason in order to realize it. When the thinker lets go his foothold on discursive thought, it is only then that he can mount to something higher.

The purpose of *śūnyatā* is beautifully put by Nāgārjuna in the following verse :

Atra brūmaḥ śūnyatāyāṁ na tvaṁ vetsi prayojanam/
Śūnyatāṁ śūnyatārthaṁ ca tata evaṁ vihanyase//
(M. K. XXIV, 7)

"You do not know the purpose of *śūnyatā*. *Śūnyatā* is not used as a theory just for the sake of *śūnyatā*." In explaining the purpose of *śunyatā*, Candrakīrti says that it is meant to silence the incessant cogitation of the verbalizing mind (*prapañcastu śūnyatāyāṁ nirudhyate*). *Śūnyatā* is taught not for its own sake, but for leading the mind to Reality by restraining its conceptualizing tendency. It is an expression of *aspiration*, not of theory.

Śūnyatā—not nihilism

It is contended by some that *śūnyatā* is sheer negativism. It denounces everything and has no positive suggestion to offer. *Śūnyatā* does not lead us anywhere. It is rank nihilism.

The Madhyamaka dialectic leading to *Śūnyatā* is not mere negativism. It does not simply negate all affirmations about Reality; it also negates all negations about Reality. It says Reality is neither *sat* (existent) nor *asat* (non-existent). It only asserts that the Absolute is inaccessible to thought; it does not say that the Absolute is a non-entity. It only maintains that the Absolute is realized in non-dual, transcendental wisdom. It vehemently pleads for the realization of the absolute Truth. Nāgārjuna says "paramārtham anāgamya nirvāṇaṁ nādhigamyate" i.e., "without realizing the absolute Truth, one cannot attain Nirvāṇa".

The Mādhyamika only negates all views about Reality; it does not negate Reality itself. It cannot, therefore, be called nihilism. As Dr. Mūrti puts it "No-doctrine, about Reality does not mean no-Reality doctrine". "*Śūnyatā* is negative only for thought; but in itself it is the non-relational knowledge of the Absolute. It may even be taken as more universal and positive than affirmation" (CPB, p. 160).

Candrakīrti vehemently protests against the Mādhyamika being called nihilist (*nāstika*). He says that the Mādhyamika only points to the relativity of things; and that his doctrine transcends both affirmation and negation (P. P. p., 156-157).

The Kārikā devotes a whole chapter (ch. XXIV) for elucidating its position that *śūnyatā* is not nihilism but only relativity and conditionedness, that it is not a rejection of the world of becoming but an explication of its inner implication viz., that the unconditioned is the ultimate truth of the conditioned. Nāgārjuna puts it beautifully in Kārikā XXIV, 14

Sarvaṁ ca yujyate tasya śūnyatā yasya yujyate||
Sarvaṁ na yujyate tasya śūnyaṁ yasya na yujyate||

"For him who accepts *śūnyatā*, everything stands in its proper place within the harmonious whole, and for him who does not accept śūnyatā, everything is out of joint."

Nāgārjuna only insists that the relative must be taken as the relative and not as the absolute and then there is proper appraisal of values and appreciation of the meaningfulness of life. His so-called negativism is only a therapeutic device.

Śūnyatā—not an end in itself

Nāgārjuna warns that one should not make a fetish of Śūnyatā. It is not an end in itself. It is only a means to lead the mind up to *prajñā* (transcendental insight), and should not be bolstered up as an end in itself. The followning verse of Nāgārjuna expresses this idea bautifully:

Śūnyatā sarvadṛṣṭīnām proktā niḥsaraṇam jinaiḥ|
Yeṣām tu śūnyatā drṣṭistān asādhyāṇ babhāṣire||

(M. K. XIII, 8)

"*Śūnyatā* was declared by the Buddha for dispensing with all views or 'isms'. Those who convert *Śūnyatā* itself into another 'ism' are verily beyond hope or help"
Chandrakīrti in commenting on the above refers to a remark of the Buddha about Śūnyatā made to Kāśyapa. The Buddha said to him "O Kāśyapa, it would be better to entertain the

personalistic view (*pudgala dṛṣṭi*) of the magnitude of mount Sumeru than to hug the *Śūnyatā* view of the nihilist (*abhāvābhiniveśikasya*). Him I call incurable who clings to *Śūnyatā* itself as a theory. If a drug administered to a patient were to remove all his disorders but were to foul the stomach itself by remaining in it, would you call the patient cured? Even so, *Śūnyatā* is an antidote against dogmatic views, but if a man were to cling to it for ever as a view in itself, he is doomed."

Elsewhere Buddha is said to have remarked that *Śūnyatā* is to be treated like a ladder for mounting up to the roof of *prajñā*. Once the roof is reached, the ladder should be discarded.

Nāgārjuna, again warns unequivocally in the following verse, against the wrong use of *Śūnyatā*.

> *Vināśayati durdṛṣṭā śūnyatā mandamedhasam/*
> *Sarpo yathā durgṛhīto vidyā vā duṣprasādhitā//*
>
> (M. K. XXIV, 11)

"Just as a snake caught at the wrong end by a dull-witted fellow only kills him or a magic wrongly employed ruins the magician, so too *Śūnyatā* wrongly used by a man who does not understand its implications only ruins him."

Dr. R. H. Robinson sums up the whole issue beautifully in the following words:

"Emptiness (śūnyatā) is not a term outside the expressional system, but is simply the key term within it. Those who would hypostatize emptiness are confusing the symbol system with the fact system." (*Early Mādhyamika in India and China*, p. 49)

Meditation on śūnyatā

It has already been said that *śūnyatā* is not simply an intellectual concept but an aspiration. In order to perfect this aspiration, one has to meditate on twenty varieties of *śūnyatā*. They are too long to be given here.

2. *Prajñāpāramitā*

The second important feature of Mahāyāna Buddhism is the practice of *prajñāpāramitā*.

Meditation on the *śūnyatā* (emptiness) is only a preparation for the spiritual discipline of *prajñāpāramitā*. *Prajñā* is super-rational. It is transcendent insight. *Prajñā* knows reality as it is (*prajñā yathābhūtam artham prajānāti*). Dr. K. V. Ramanan says that *Mahāprajñā pāramitā Śāstra* uses the world *prajñā* in two senses, viz. (1) the eternal *prajñā*, and (2) the *prajñā* that functions along with the five *pāramitās*. The latter is the functional *prajñāpāramitā*, while the former is the substantial or stable *prajñā*. The functional *prajñā* puts an end to the darkness of ignorance and thus the eternal *prajñā* comes to the fore. In the eternal *prajñā*, one cannot find even the distinction of ignorance and knowledge. It is an ever-present luminous knowledge. It is the "eternal light in the heart of man." Particular objects arise and perish, but the light of this *prajñā* keeps for ever shining.

The functional *prajñā* is the act of knowing which consists of analysis, criticism and comprehension. These are only mode of the power of the permanent *prajñā*.

It is only by attaining *prajñā* that we can know Truth. *Prajñā* cannot be attained by the chattering academician 'sicklied over with the pale cast of thought', nor can it be attained simply by putting on the wishing cap. It can be attained only by arduous self-discipline and self-culture. *Prajñāpāramitā* is usually translated as perfection of wisdom, but it really means 'transcendent wisdom' (*prajñā pāramitā*).

There are six spiritual qualities that have to be acquired. Prajñāpāramitā is a blanket term for all these qualities. They are 1. *dāna* (charity) 2. *śila* (withdrawing from all evil deeds), 3. *kṣānti* (forbearance), 4. *vīrya* (enthusiasm and exertion), 5. *dhyāna* (concentration) 6. *prajñā* (transcendental insight). The first four are moral qualities. Their development prepares one for the practice of *dhyāna*. *Dhyāna* orients the mind towards *prajñā*. After sufficient practice of *dhyāna*, scales fall from the eyes and one sees truth face to face (*vipaśyanā*); the chrysalis of the ego is split asunder, and one sees 'the light that never was on sea or land' :

The object of *prajñāpāramitā* is *tathatā*, *dharmadhātu*, *bhūtakoṭī*

Prajñāpāramitā is the highest kind of knowledge. It is an integral principle which comprehends both the aspects of cognition and emotion and so comprises both truth and universal love. It destroys not only the craving for sense-pleasure but also all desire for power and pelf.

3. *The Ideal of the Bodhisattva*

It has already been said in connexion with the distinction between Hīnayāna and Mahāyāna that the attainment of the status of the Bodhisattva is the ideal of Mahāyāna.

According to the *Mahāprajñāpāramitā-śāstra*, Bodhi means the way of all the Buddhas, and *sattva* means the essence and character of the good *dharma*. The *citta* of the Bodhisattva helps every one to cross the stream of birth and death. Therefore it is the *citta* or the individual that is really the Bodhisattva.

There are three important qualities of the Bodhisattva, viz, the great resolve to save all mankind, the thought that is unshakable, and the effort that knows no set-back.

When an aspirant acquires *anutpattika-dharma-kṣānti* i.e. the capacity to endure and sustain the truth of the unborn *dharma*, then he enters the true status (*nyāma*) of the Bodhisattva. Having entered this status, he is known as *avaivarta*, the irreversible, the unshakable.

When he realizes the *anutpattika-dharma-kṣānti*, he puts an end to the *kleśas* and when he achieves Buddhahood, he puts an end to their residual impressions.

The aspirant evolves to the status of a Bodhisattva by *anuttara pūjā*—a devotional discipline consisting of seven steps, and the practice of the six *prajñāpāramitās*. The highest development of the Bodhisattva consists in acquiring *bodhicitta* which has two aspects, viz. (1) *Śūnyatā* or *prajñā* and, (2) *Karuṇā*. We have already seen what *śūnyatā* or *prajñā* is. *Karuṇā* is usually translated as compassion or commiseration, but it is better to translate it as universal love as Suzuki has done. *Prajñā* or transcendent wisdom and *Karuṇā* or universal love constitute Buddhahood.

4. *Buddhology*

In Hīnayāna, the Buddha was simply a human being who by his own effort became enlightened and divine. In Mahāyāna, it is Divinity itself that incarnates itself in a Buddha and descends to earth to impart the highest teaching about man's destiny as an act of grace.

Mahāyāna evolved the concept of three bodies of the Buddha, viz. (1) *Nirmāṇa-kāya* (2) *Dharma-kāya* and (3) *Sambhoga-kāya.* The *Sambhoga-kāya* or the body of bliss was a concept evolved later by the Yogācārins. The Mādhyamikas speak only of two bodies of the Buddha, viz. *Dharma-kāya* and *Nirmāṇa-kāya.*

Dharma is a most protean word in Buddhism. In the broadest sense it means an impersonal spiritual energy behind and in everything. There are four important senses in which this word has been used in Buddhist philosophy and religion.

(1) *Dharma* in the sense of one ultimate Reality. It is both transcendent and immanent to the world, and also the governing law within it.

(2) *Dharma* in the sense of scripture, doctrine, religion, as the Buddhist *dharma.*

(3) *Dharma* in the sense of righteousness, virtue, piety.

(4) *Dharma* in the sense of "elements of existence." In this sense, it is generally used in plural.

Dharma in the word *Dharma-kāya* is used in the first sense, viz. ultimate Reality. The word *kāya* in this context is not used in the literal sense of body, but in the sense of *āśraya* or substratum, in the sense of unity, organised form. Dharmakāya means 'the principle of cosmic unity'. It is not merely an abstract philosophical concept, but an 'object of the religious consciousness'.

Dharmakāya

Dharma is the essence of being, the ultimate Reality, the Absolute. The *Dharma-kāya* is the essential nature of the Buddha. As Dharmakāya, the Buddha experiences his identity with Dharma or the Absolute and his unity (*samatā*) with all beings. The Dharmakāya is a knowing; loving, willing being, an inexhaustible fountain-head of love and compassion.

When Buddha's disciple, the monk Vakkali was on his death-bed, he expressed his ardent desire to see the Buddha in person. On that occasion, the Buddha remarked "He who sees the *Dhamma* sees Me. He who sees Me sees the *Dhamma.*"

This statement of the Buddha gave rise to the conviction that the real Buddha was the *Dharma*, not the historical Gautama known as the Buddha, and thus the idea of *Dharma-kāya* was developed. The Mahāsaṅghikas conceived of Buddha as *lokottara* or *Dharma-kāya* (transcendental) and Śākyamuni only as *Nirmāṇakāya* or a phantom body conjured up by the *Dharma-kāya* for bringing the message of *Dharma* to ignorant humanity.

Dharma-kāya is the essential transcendental aspect of the Buddha. Dharmatā is the ultimate impersonal principle. Dharma-kāya is the ultimate universal person. There is a slight resemblance between the *Brahman* and *Īśvara* of Vedānta and Dharmadhātu and *Dharma-kāya* of the Mādhyamika. *Dharma dhātu* or *tathatā is* like the Vedāntic Brahman and *Dharma-kāya* is something like the Vedāntic *Īśvara*, but there is also a good deal of difference between the two. In Vedānta, *Īśvara* in association with *Māyā* creates, sustains and withdraws the universe. *Dharma-kāya* has no such function. The function of *Dharma-kāya* is to descend out of his deep wisdom and love, to earth as a Buddha in order to teach the *Dharma* and uplift erring humanity. He is Divine and yet not God, for in every system the function of creation of the universe is associated with God. Buddhism does not believe in any such God. Suzuki puts the idea of God in Buddhism in the following words: "Buddhism must not be judged as an atheism which endorses an agnostic, materialistic interpretation of the universe. Far from it, Buddhism outspokenly acknowledges the presence in the world of a reality which transcends the limitations of phenomenality, but which is nevertheless immanent everywhere and manifests itself in its full glory, and in which we live, and move and have our being." (*Outlines of Mahāyāna Buddhism* p. 219)

Dharma-kāya is identified with the Absolute and is also connected with the phenomenal. Therefore it is Dharma-kāya alone that can descend to earth as the saviour of mankind.

Whenever Dharmakāya decides to come down to earth in human form, He conjures up a phantom body called *Nirmāṇa-kāya*. *Nirmāṇa-kāya* is the body assumed by *Dharma-kāya* whenever he decides to come down to earth to save mankind. It is through this that He incarnates in a human form, as a Buddha, as the saviour of mankind. The actual physical body of the Buddha is the *Rūpa-kāya*. It will thus be seen that Buddhism is not a historical religion like official Christianity. The Buddha is not the founder of a religion. He only transmits Dharma which is eternal. There have been many Buddhas before, and there will be many Buddhas in the future.

When a Buddhist takes refuge in the Buddha, it is the eternal *Dharma-kāya Buddha* in whom he takes refuge.

Nirmāṇa-Kāya

It has already been said that *Nirmāṇa-kāya* is a body assumed by the Buddha in order to establish contact with the world in a human form. *Dharma-kāya* is also known as *Svābhāvika-kāya* or the essential, natural *kāya* of the Buddha. The *Nirmāṇakāya* is assumed for the time being for a specific purpose. The *Rūpa-kāya* or the actual physical body of the Buddha is visible to every one. The *Nirmāṇa-kāya* is visible only to adepts.

Significance of the Concept of Madhyamā Pratipad

The Buddha used to say that Truth did not lie in the extreme alternatives but in the middle position (*madhyamā pratipad*). Hīnayānists generally used the concept of *madhyamā pratipad* in the ethical sense, in the sense of neither taking too much food nor too little, neither sleeping too much, nor too little etc.

The Mādhyamikas interpreted *madhyamā pratipad* in a metaphysical sense also. Says Nāgārjuna:

Kātyāyanāvavāde cāstīti nāstīti cobhayam |
Pratiṣiddhaṁ bhagavatā bhāvābhāvavibhāvinā ||
(M. K. XV, 7)

"In the *Kātyāyanāvavāda-sūtra*, the Lord who had the right insight into both *bhāva* (ens) and *abhāva* (non-ens) rejected both the extreme alternatives of 'is' and 'is not."

In commenting on this, Candrakīrti has quoted the relevant passage in the *Kātyāyanāvavāda-sūtra* which is accepted as an authority by all the Buddhists. In this, Buddha says to Kāśyapa, "O Kāśyapa, 'is' is one extreme alternative, 'not is' is another extreme alternative. That which is the *madhyama* position is intangible, incomparable, without any position, non-appearing, incomprehensible. That is what is meant by *madhyamā pratipat* (the middle position) O Kāśyapa. It is perception of Reality (*bhūta pratyavekṣā*)" (P. P., p. 118) Nāgārjuna takes his stand on this authoritative statement of the Buddha. The word *madhyama* is not to be taken in its literal sense of 'in between' or a 'mean between the two'. As is clear from the adjectives 'intangible, incomparable, incomprehensible etc., *madhyamā pratipat* (the middle position) means that Reality is transcendent to the antinomies of Reason, the dichotomies of thought, and cannot be 'cabined, caged and confined' in the alternatives of 'is' and 'is not'. It is on this basis that Nāgārjuna called his philosophy *madhyamaka* i.e. 'pertaining to the transcendent'.

Extremes become the dead-ends of eternalism and annihilationalism. There are those who cling exclusively to nonbeing and there are others who cling exclusively to being. The great Buddha meant, by his doctrine of *madhyamā pratipat* (Middle way), to drive home the truth that things here are neither absolute being nor absolute non-being, but are arising and perishing, forming continuous becoming, and that Reality is transcendent to thought and cannot be caught up in the dichotomies of the mind.

The Absolute and Phenomena

There are many words used for the Absolute or Reality in Madhyamaka philosophy. *Tathatā* (suchness) *śūnyatā*, *nirvāṇa*, *advaya* (non-dual), *anutpanna* (unproduced), *nirvikalpa* (the realm of non-discrimination), *dharmdhātu* or *dharmatā* (the essence of being, the true nature of Dharma), *anabhilāpya* (the inexpressible) *tattva* (thatness) *niśprapañca* (free of verbalisation and plurality), *yathābhūta* (that which really is), *Satya* (Truth), *bhūtatathatā* or *bhūtatā* (the true reality), *tathāgata-garbha* (the womb of Tathāgatas), *aparapratyaya* (reality which one must realize within oneself), etc. Each word is used from a particular standpoint.

Throughout the *Madhyamaka śāstra*, Nāgārjuna has been at pains to prove that the Absolute is transcendent to both thought and speech. Neither the concept of *bhāva* (ens) nor *abhāva* (non-ens) is applicable to it. Nāgārjuna advances the following reason for the inapplicability of these concepts.

Bhāvastāvad na nirvāṇaṁ jarāmaraṇalakṣaṇam |
Prasajyetāsti bhāvo hi na jarāmaraṇaṁ vinā ||

(M. K. XXV 4)

"Nirvāṇa or the Absolute Reality cannot be a *bhāva* or positive ens, for in that case it would be subject to origination, decay, and death; there is no empirical existence which is free from decay and death. If it cannot be *bhāva*, far less can it be *abhāva*, (non-existence), for *abhāva* (non-existence) is only a relative concept (absence of *bhāva*) depending upon the concept of *bhāva*." As Nāgārjuna puts it:

Bhāvasya cedaprasiddhirabhāvo naiva siddhyati |
Bhāvasya hyanyathābhāvam abhāvam bruvate janāḥ ||

(M. K. XV, 5)

"When *bhāva* itself is proved to be inapplicable to Reality, *abhāva* cannot stand scrutiny, for *abhāva* is known only as the disappearance of *bhāva*."

When the concepts of *bhāva* (empirical existence), and *abhāva* (the negation of *bhāva*) cannot be applied to the Absolute, the question of applying any other concept to it does not arise, for all other concepts depend upon the above two. In one word, the Absolute is transcendent to thought, and because it is transcendent to thought, it is inexpressible.

Nirvṛttamabhidhātavyaṁ nivṛtte cittagocare |
Anutpannāniruddhā hi nirvāṇamiva dharmatā ||

(XVIII, 7)

"What cannot be an object of thought cannot, *a fortiori*, be an object of speech. The Absolute as the essence of all being is neither born, nor does it cease to be."

Candrakīrti says, *Paramārtho hi āryāṇām tūṣṇīmbhāvaḥ* (P. P. p. 19) "To the saints, the Absolute is just silence i.e. it is inexpressible".

Phenomena have no independent, substantial reality of their own. Relativity or dependence is the main characteristic of phenomena, and that which is relative is not real in the highest sense of the word. The Absolute is the Reality of the appearances.

The Absolute and the world are not two different sets of reality posited against each other. Phenomena viewed as relative, as governed by causes and conditions constitute the world, and viewed as free of all conditions are the Absolute.

The Absolute is always of uniform nature. Nirvāṇa or the Absolute Reality is not something produced or achieved. Nirvāṇa only means the disappearance of the fabrications of discursive thought.

If the Absolute is beyond all thought and speech, how can the Absolute be described, how can there be any teaching about the Absolute? The answer is—Phenomena do not completely cut us off from Reality. Phenomena are appearances, and appearances point to their Reality. The veil gives a hint of that which is veiled.

Candrakīrti quotes a saying of the Buddha,

Anakṣarasya dharmasya śrutiḥ kā deśanā ca kā |
Śrūyate deśyate cāpi samāropādanakṣaraḥ ||

"How can there be any understanding or teaching of that which is wordless (i.e. inexpressible)? That can be understood and taught only by *samāropa*—an ascribed mark." Phenomena serve as the 'ascribed mark' of Reality. Phenomena are like an envelope that contains within it an invitation from Reality. The superimposed character (*samāropa*) of phenomena veils the noumenon; when that superimposed character is uncovered, when the veil is removed, it only reveals Reality. The philosophy of *Śūnyatā* is meant only to help uncover the veil.

Saṁvṛti and Paramārtha Satya

Are phenomena wholly unreal? Nāgārjuna says they have reality of a sort. They are *saṁvṛti satya*; they are the *appearance* of Reality. Appearance points to that which appears. *Saṁvṛti* is appearance, cover or veil. *Saṁvṛti* or cover is not a mere gossamer floating about in *vacuo*; *saṁvṛti* covers *paramārtha* (absolute reality). Nāgārjuna says:

Dve satye samupāśritya buddhānāṁ dharmadeśanā |
Lokasaṁvṛtisatyaṁ ca satyaṁ ca paramārthataḥ ||

(M. K., XXIV, 8)

"The Buddhas teach the *Dharma* by resorting to two truths, *saṁvṛti-satya* (empirical truth) and *paramārtha-satya* (absolute truth)."

So important is the distinction that Nāgārjuna maintains that no one can understand the teaching of the Buddha who does not know this distinction.

Ye 'nayor na vijānanti vibhāgaṁ satyayor dvayoḥ |
Te tattvaṁ na vijānanti gambhīraṁ Buddhaśāsane ||

(M. K. XXIV, 9)

"Those who do not know the distinction between these two truths cannot understand the deep significance of the teaching of the Buddha."

Candrakīrti explains *saṁvṛti* in the following way:

Samantādvaraṇam saṁvṛtiḥ. Ajñānaṁ hi samantāt-sarva-padārthatattvāvacchādanāt saṁvṛtirityucyate ||

(P. P. p. 215)

"That which covers all round is *saṁvṛti. Saṁvṛti* is *ajñāna* (primal ignorance) which covers the real nature of all things." Phenomena are characterized as *saṁvṛti,* because they throw a veil over Reality. At the same time they serve as a pointer to Reality as their ground. *Saṁvṛti-satya* is *vyāvahārika-satya* .. pragmatic or empirical reality. *Paramārtha-satya* is absolute reality. Two truths—*Saṁvṛti*-and *paramārtha*, however, do not connote two different spheres to which they are applied. The Absolute comprehended through the categories of thought is phenomena and phenomena stripped of these categories are the Absolute.

Candrakīrti mentions three senses of *saṁvṛti*

(1) *Samantāt sarvapadārthatattvāvacchādanāt saṁvṛtiḥ.*

(P. p. p. 215)

Saṁvṛti is that which covers all round the real nature of things. Candrakīrti calls it *ajñāna* (the primal ignorance). *Saṁvṛti* is due to *ajñāna* or *avidyā* and is identical with it. It is the primal ignorance that throws a veil over Reality.

(2) *Parasparasambhavanaṁ vā saṁvṛtiranyonyasamāśrayeṇa*

(P. p. p. 215)

Saṁvṛti is mutual dependence of things or their relativity. In this sense, it is identical with phenomena.

(3) *Saṁvṛtiḥ saṁketo lokavyavahāraḥ. Sa ca abhidhānābhidheya-jñānajñeyādilakṣaṇaḥ.*

(P. p. p. 215)

What is conventionally accepted by people at large is *saṁvṛti.*

All these senses are mutually connected. The first one is the primary sense, but each of these senses has an importance from the point of view of empirical reality.

Saṁvṛti or pragmatic reality is the means (*upāya*) for reaching

Reality which is the goal (*upeya*). Nāgārjuna expressly mentions the importance of *vyavahāra* or empirical reality in attaining *paramārtha* or absolute reality. Says he:

Vyavahāramanāśritya paramārtho na deśyate |
Paramārthamanāgamya nirvāṇaṁ nādhigamyate ||

(M. K. XXIV, 10)

"Without a recourse to pragmatic reality, the absolute truth cannot be taught. Without knowing the absolute truth, *nirvāṇa* cannot be attained."

Commenting on this, Candrakīrti says:

Tasmād nirvāṇādhigamopāyatvād avaśyameva yathāvasthitā saṁvṛtiḥ ādāveva abhyupeyā bhājanam iva salilārthinā ||

(P. P. P. 216)

"Therefore, inasmuch as *saṁvṛti* as characterized is a means for the attainment of Nirvāṇa, it should, be adopted, just as a pot is to be used by one desirous of water." *Saṁvṛti* is *upāya* (means), *paramārtha* is *upeya* (goal).

There are two kinds of *saṁvṛti*—(i) *loka-saṁvṛti* and (ii) *aloka-saṁvṛti.* (i) *Loka-saṁvṛti* refers to the common empirical objects recognized as real by all as for example, a jar, a piece of cloth etc, (ii) *Aloka saṁvṛti* refers to objects experienced under abnormal conditions. Illusory objects, distorted perceptions caused by diseased or defective sense-organs, dream objects etc. are cases of *aloka-saṁvṛti.* These are *aloka-saṁvṛti*—non-empirical, for they are unreal even for the empirical consciousness.

Prajñākaramati has designated *loka-saṁvṛti* as *tathya-saṁvṛti* (true *saṁvṛti*) and *aloka-saṁvṛti* as *mithyā-saṁvṛti* (false *saṁvṛti*). The former is like the *vyāvahārika sattā*, and the latter like the *prātibhāsika sattā* of the Vedāntists—Just as *aloka-saṁvṛti* is unreal for the empirical consciousness, even so *loka-saṁvṛti* is unreal from the transcendental point of view. *Saṁvṛti* is called *satya* (true or real) by courtesy, for there cannot be degrees in Truth. Paramārtha or the Absolute Reality alone is truly real.

The texts or teachings of the Buddha bearing on *paramārtha satya* or the Absolute Reality are called *nītārtha* (primary or direct) and those bearing on *saṁvṛti-satya* are called *neyārtha* (secondary, indirect) by the Mādhyamika.

Tathatā-Tathāgata

We have seen that *dharma-dhātu* or *dharmatā* or *tathatā* is the word used in Madhyamaka philosophy for the Absolute. Candrakīrti says, *Yā sā dharmāṇāṁ dharmatā nāma saiva tatsvarūpam* (P. P. p. 116). "That which is the essential being of all elements of existence is the nature of Reality." It is *tathatā*, it is Reality such as it is. In the words of Bradley, we can only say *that* it is, not *what* it is. According to Candrakīrti—*tathābhāvo'vikāritvaṁ sadaiva sthāyitā.* (P. P. p. 116) "The thatness of Reality consists in its invariability, in its remaining for ever as it is."

Tathatā is the Truth, but it is impersonal. In order to reveal itself, it requires a medium. Tathāgata is that medium. Tathāgata is the epiphany of Reality. He is Reality personalized. Tathāgata is an amphibious being partaking both of the Absolute and phenomena. He is identical with Tathatā, but embodied in a human form. That is why Tathatā is also called Tathāgatagarbha (the womb of Tathāgata).

The word Tathāgata is interpreted as *tathā+gata* or *tathā+āgata* i.e. 'thus gone' or 'thus come' i.e. as the previous Buddhas have come and gone. This, however, does not throw much light on the concept of Tathāgata. There is one verse in the *Mahābhārata* which, it seems to me, removes completely the obscurity surrounding this word.

> Śakuntānāmivākāśe matsyānāmiva codake /
> Padaṁ yathā na dṛśyate *tathā* jñānavidāṁ *gatiḥ* //
>
> (*Śāntiparva*, 181, 12)

"Just as the foot-prints of birds flying in the sky and of fish swimming in water may not be seen: *So or thus* is the *going* of those who have realized the Truth."

This very word *tathā-gati* (only a different form of *tathāgata*) is used for those perfect beings whose foot-prints are untraceable. The word 'untraceable' is used for Tathāgata in *Majjhimanikāya*, Vol. I, p. 140, P. T. S. ed. *tathāgatam ananuvejjoti vadāmi* i.e. 'I declare that Tathāgata is *ananuvejja* (skt-*ananuvedya*) i. e. whose track is untraceable, who is above all the dichotomies of thought.' In the *Dhammapada* also, the Buddha has been called *apada* (trackless) in *tam Buddhamananta-*

gocaram apadaṁ kena padena nessatha (verse 179). Again in the verse 254 of the *Dhammapada*, the word Tathāgata has been used in connexion with *ākāse padaṁ natthi*. It appears that Tathāgata only means 'thus gone' 'so gone' i.e. trackless, whose track cannot be traced, by any of the categories of thought.

The *Mahābhārata* is considered by some scholars to be pre-Buddhistic. Whether it is pre-Buddhistic or post-Buddhistic, *tathāgata* seems to have been used for those who had realized Truth and were trackless.

Whatever the origin of the word, the function of Tathāgata is clear. He descends on earth to impart the light of Truth to mankind and departs without any track. He is the embodiment of Tathatā. When the Buddha is called *Tathāgata*, his individual personality is ignored; he is treated as a 'type' that appears from time to time in the world. He is the earthly manifestation of *Dharma*. The *Tathāgata* who has gone beyond all plurality and categories of thought (*sarvaprapañca-atīta*) can be said to be neither permanent nor impermanent. He is untraceable. Permanent and impermanent can be applied only where there is duality, not in the case of the non-dual. And because *Tathatā* is the same in all manifestation, therefore all beings are potential *Tathāgatas*. It is the *Tathāgata* within us who makes us long for *Nirvāṇa* and ultimately sets us free.

Śūnyatā and *Karuṇā* are the essential characteristics of *Tathāgata*. *Śūnyatā* in this context means *prajñā* (transcendental insight). Having *Śūnyatā* or *prajñā*, Tathāgata is identical with *Tathatā* or *Śūnya*. Having *karuṇā*, he is the saviour of all sentient beings.

The true being of the Tathāgata which is also the true being of all is not conceivable. In his ultimate nature, the Tathāgata is "deep, immeasurable, unfathomable."

The *dharmas* or elements of existence are indeterminable, because they are conditioned, because they are relative. The Tathāgata is indeterminable in a different sense. The Tathāgata is indeterminable, because, in his ultimate nature, he is not conditionally born. The indeterminability of the ultimate nature really means 'the inapplicability of the ways of concepts.' Nāgārjuna puts it beautifully in this Karikā;

Prapañcayanti ye Buddham prapañcātītam avyayam |
Te prapañcahatāḥ sarve na paśyanti Tathāgatam || (XXII, 15)

"Those who describe the Buddha who is transcendent to thought and word and is not subject to birth and death in terms of conceptual categories are all victims of *prapañca* (the verbalising mind) and are thus unable to see the Tathāgata in his real nature."

Candrakīrti quotes a verse from *Vajracchedikā* (verse 43) :

Dharmato Buddhā draṣṭavyā dharmakāyā hi nāyakāḥ /
Dharmatā cāpyavijñeyā na sā śakyā vijānitum //

(P. P., p. 195)

"The Buddhas are to be seen in their real *dharma*-nature, for these supreme guides (of humanity) have the *dharma*-nature in their core. But the essence of *dharma* is transcendent to thought and cannot be grasped by ideation."

The *tathatā* or the unconditioned Reality is not another entity *apart* from the conditioned. The unconditioned is the ground of the conditioned. To think that the determinate things are ultimate and self-existent in their distinct natures is to commit the error of eternalism śāśvata-vāda), and to think that the indeterminate or the unconditioned is wholly exclusive of the determinate is to commit the error of negativism.

The *Mahāprajñāpāramitā Śāstra* distinguishes three kinds of *tathatā* or essential nature. The first consists of the specific, distinct nature of every thing, the second of the non-ultimacy of the specific natures of things, of the conditionedness or relativity of all things that are determinate, and the third of the ultimate reality of every thing. Actually, however, the first two are called *tathatā* only by courtesy. It is only the ultimate, unconditioned nature of all that appears which is *tathatā* in the highest sense.

Tathatā or the "true nature' of things at the different levels, viz., mundane or appearance and transmundane or Reality is also called *dharmatā* at the two different levels.

DHARMADHĀTU AND BHŪTAKOṬI

Tathatā or Reality is also called Nirvāṇa or *dharmatā* or *dharmadhātu*. The word *dhātu* in this context means the inmost nature, the ultimate essence.

The *tathatā* or *dharmadhātu* is both transcendent and immanent. It is transcendent as ultimate Reality, but it is present in every one as his inmost ground and essence.

Bhūtakoṭi refers to the skilful penetration of the mind into the *dharmadhātu.* The word 'bhūta' means the unconditioned reality, the *dharmadhātu*: The word 'Koṭi' means the skill to reach the limit or the end ; it signifies realization. Bhūtakoṭi is also called *anutpādakoṭi*, which means the end beyond birth and death.

All things mentally analysed and tracked to their source are seen to enter the *anutpādadharma*, the *dharmadhātu.* This entering of all things into the unconditioned Reality is known as *anutpādakoṭi*, *anutpāda* signifies Nirvāṇa which is beyond birth and death. In the *dharmadhātu*, all beings are transformed into the dharma nature.

Prajñāpāramitā is equated with *dharmadhātu. Advaya— the non-dual* or *undivided.*

According to Madhyamaka philosophy, Reality is non-dual. The essential conditionedness of entities, when properly understood, reveals the unconditioned as not only as their ground but also as the ultimate reality of the conditioned entities themselves. In fact, the conditioned and the unconditioned are not two, not separate. This is only a relative distinction, not an absolute division. That is why Nāgārjuna says, "What from one point of view is *saṁsāra* is from another point of view Nirvāṇa itself."

(XXV, 20)

We have seen the main features of Madhyamaka philosophy. It is both philosophy and mysticism. By its dialectic, its critical probe (*prasaṅgāpādana*) into all the categories of thought, it relentlessly exposes the pretensions of Reason to know Truth. The hour of Reason's despair, however, becomes the hour of Truth. The seeker now turns to meditation on the various forms of *śūnyatā*, and the practice of *prajñāpāramitās.* By moral and yogic practices, he is prepared to receive the Truth. In the final stage of *Prajñā*, the wheels of imagination are stopped, the discursive mind is stilled, and in that silence Reality (*bhūta-tathatā*) stoops to kiss the eye of the aspirant; he receives the accolade of *prajñā* and becomes the knight-errant of Truth. There is no greater certainty than that of the mystic and equally there is no greater impotence laid upon him in giving expression to the Truth which he has received on that dizzy summit of experience. It is an experience of a different dimension-spaceless, timeless, *nirvikalpa* (beyond the province of thought and speech) Hence it cannot be expressed in any human language. The question is put at the logical level of Reason; the answer is found at the supralogical, suprarational level of *prajñā* which one can mount to only by a life of moral and spiritual discipline. The Madhyamaka system is neither scepticism nor agnosticism. It is an open invitation to every one to see Reality face to face.

We saw at the outset that the ideal of Mahāyāna is the Bodhisattva. We shall conclude this brief summary of Madhyamaka system with the following words of Saṅgharakshita: "Buddhism may be compared to a tree. Buddha's transcendental realization is the root. The basic Buddhism is the trunk, the distinctive Mahāyāna doctrines the branches, and the schools and sub-schools of the Mahāyāna the flowers. Now the function of flowers, however beautiful, is to produce fruit. Philosophy, to be more than mere barren speculation, must find its reason and its fulfilment in a way of life; thought should lead to action. Doctrine gives birth to Method. The Bodhisattva ideal is the perfectly ripened fruit of the whole vast tree of Buddhism. Just as the fruit encloses the seed, so within the Bodhisattva Ideal are recombined all the different and sometimes seemingly divergent elements of Mahāyāna" (*A Survey of Buddhism*, p. 432).

INDEX